The Poetry of

A Critical Study Guide

Edited by Mungo Parks M.Litt

Olympia Harbour Inc.

Tinfish Type - Librarie du Levant 2022 – Marlinspike 35451

Olympia Harbour Publications Inc.
Marlinspike Building, Marlinspike Place, Greenwich Conn.

The Poetry of John Donne – A Critical Study Guide

Contents   page

Introduction   5
Biography   7
The Metaphysical Poets   9
Songs and Sonnets   10
Style   11

Air and Angels   13
The Anniversary   16
The Apparition   19
The Canonization   20
The Flea   26
The Good Morrow   31
Woman's Constancy   34
To His Mistress Going to Bed   36
A Jet Ring Sent   41
The Relic   43
The Sun Rising   48
The Triple Fool   51
Twicknam Garden   53
A Valediction Forbidding Mourning   56
A Valediction of Weeping   60
Elegy V: His Picture   63
Song: Go and Catch a Falling Star   65
Song: Sweetest Love, I Do Not Go   67
A Nocturnal Upon St Lucy's Day   69
A Hymn to God the Father   72
The Indifferent   74
The Holy Sonnets   75

I: Thou Hast Made Me, Shall Thy Work Decay?	76
V: I Am A Little World Made Cunningly	78
VI: This is My Play's Last Scene	79
VII: At the Round Earth's Imagined Corners . . .	81
X: Death, Be Not Proud	82
XI: Spit in My Face You Jews . . .	83
XIV: Batter My Heart, Three-Person'd God	85
Donne's Timeline	87
Exam Advice	88
Exam Questions	89
Model Essay	90
Creative Tasks	93
Glossary	94
Donne's Reputation	97
Donne's Amatory Poems	98
The Mind of John Donne	100
Donne's Career	103
Donne's Poetry and Prose	104
Biographies on Donne	112
Bibliography	113

This study guide is designed to support a student's reading of John Donne's poetry. It includes a commentary for each poem as well as notes on the historical context and the major themes running through his work. There is also a section with essay questions, how to respond in an AQA or Edexcel A Level exam, the selected thoughts of contemporary critics, and a comprehensive glossary.

Introduction

Other poets have known as much of people's hearts, but John Donne, partly by his very method of saying things, is able to render exactly, and with such elaborate subtlety, every passionate mood known to man. Donne, as he suffers all the colds and fevers of love, is as much the sufferer and the physician of his disease as he was when recording cases of actual physical sickness. Always detached from himself, even when he is most helplessly the slave of circumstances, he has that faculty of seeing through his own illusions. Other poets, with more wisdom towards poetry, give us the beautiful or pathetic results of creeping or soaring passions. Donne, making a new thing certainly, if not always a thing of beauty, tells us exactly what a man really feels as he makes love to a woman, as he sits beside her husband at table, as he dreams of her in absence, as he scorns himself for loving her, as he hates or despises her for loving him, as he realises all that is doubtful in her devotion, and all that is animal in his. 'Nature's lay idiot, I taught thee to love,' he tells her, in a burst of angry contempt, priding himself on his superior craft in the art. And his devotions to her are exquisite, appealing to what is most responsive in woman. Donne arguably shows women themselves, in delight, anger, or despair, and we know that he finds nothing in the world more interesting.

Both reason and passion then speak in the quintessence of Donne's verse with an exalted simplicity which seems to make a new language for love. It is the simplicity of a perfectly abstract geometrical problem, solved by one to whom the rapture of solution is the blossoming of pure reason. *The Canonization*, for example, anticipates a metaphysical Blake yet it is exactly what its title claims to be.

Furthermore, in the poems of divine love there is the same quality of mental emotion as in the poems of human love. Donne adores God reasonably, knowing why he adores Him. He renders thanks point by point, celebrates the heavenly perfections with metaphysical precision, and is no vaguer with God than with woman. Donne knew what he believed and why he believed, and is carried into no heat or mist as he tells over the recording rosary of his devotions.

But for the writing of great poetry something more is needed than to be a poet and to have a faith or great occasions. Donne was a poet, and he had the passions and the passionate adventures, in body and mind, which make the material for poetry; he was sincere to himself in expressing what he really felt under the burden of strong emotion and sharp sensation. It is always useful to remember Wordsworth's phrase of 'emotion recollected in tranquillity,' for nothing so well defines that moment of crystallisation in which direct emotion or sensation deviates exquisitely into art.

Donne is intent on the passion itself, the thought, the reality; so intent that he is not at the same time, in that half-unconscious way which is the way of the really great poet, equally intent on the form, that both may come to ripeness together. Again it is the heresy of the realist. Just as he drags into his verse words that have had no time to take colour from men's association of them with beauty, so he puts his 'naked thinking heart' into verse as if he were setting forth an argument. He gives us the real thing, as he would have been proud to assure us. But poetry will have nothing to do with real things, until it has translated them into a diviner world. That world may be as closely the pattern of ours as the worlds which Dante saw in hell and purgatory; the language of the poet may be as close to the language of daily speech as the supreme poetic language of Dante. But the personal or human reality and the imaginative or divine reality must be perfectly interfused, or the art will be at fault. Donne is too proud to abandon himself to his own inspiration, to his inspiration as a poet; he would be something more than a voice for deeper yet speechless powers; he would make poetry speak straight.

Biography

John Donne was born in Bread Street, London on January 22, 1572 to Catholic parents. His father was a well-to-do ironmonger who died suddenly in 1576, and left the three children to be raised by their mother, Elizabeth, who was the daughter of epigrammatist and playwright John Heywood and a relative of Sir Thomas More.

Donne is known as the founder of the Metaphysical Poets, a term created by Samuel Johnson, an eighteenth-century English essayist and philosopher. The loosely associated group also includes George Herbert, Andrew Marvell, and John Cleveland. The Metaphysical Poets are known for their ability to startle the reader and coax new perspective through paradoxical images, subtle argument, inventive syntax, and imagery from art, philosophy, and religion using an extended metaphor known as a conceit. Donne reached beyond the rational and hierarchical structures of the seventeenth century with his exacting and ingenious conceits, advancing the exploratory spirit of his time.

Donne entered the world during a period of theological and political unrest for both England and France; a Protestant massacre occurred on Saint Bartholomew's day in France; while in England, the Catholics were the persecuted minority. Born into a Roman Catholic family, Donne's personal relationship with religion was tumultuous and passionate, and at the centre of much of his poetry. He studied at Hart Hall, Oxford for three years and then at Cambridge for another three years. He did not take a degree at either university, because to do so would have meant taking the Oath of Supremacy, which identified the reigning monarch as the head of the Church in England. At the age of twenty he studied law at Lincoln's Inn. Two years later, in 1593, he succumbed to religious pressure and joined the Anglican Church after his younger brother, Henry, died of a fever in prison, having been arrested for giving a Catholic priest sanctuary. Donne wrote most of his love lyrics, erotic verse, and some sacred poems in the 1590s, creating two major volumes of work: *Satires* and *Songs and Sonnets*.

In 1598, after returning from a two-year naval expedition against Spain, Donne was appointed private secretary to Sir Thomas Egerton. While sitting in Queen Elizabeth's last Parliament in 1601, Donne, aged twenty-nine, secretly married Anne More, the sixteen-year-old niece of Lady Egerton. Donne's father-in-law disapproved of the marriage. As punishment, he did not provide a dowry for the couple and had Donne briefly imprisoned.

This left the couple isolated and dependent on friends, relatives, and patrons. Donne suffered social and financial instability in the years following his marriage, exacerbated by the birth of many children. He continued to write and published the *Divine Poems* in 1607. In *Pseudo-Martyr*, published in 1610, Donne displayed his extensive knowledge of the laws of the Church and state, arguing that Roman Catholics could support James I without compromising their faith. In 1615, James I pressured him to enter the Anglican Ministry by declaring that Donne could not be employed outside of the Church. He was appointed Royal Chaplain later that year. His wife died in 1617 at thirty-three years old shortly after giving birth to their twelfth child, who was stillborn. The *Holy Sonnets* are also attributed to this phase of his life.

In 1621, he became dean of Saint Paul's Cathedral. In his later years, Donne's writing reflected his fear of his inevitable death. He wrote his private prayers, *Devotions upon Emergent Occasions*, during a period of severe illness and published them in 1624. His learned, charismatic, and inventive preaching made him a highly influential presence in London. Best known for his vivacious, compelling style and thorough examination of mortal paradox, John Donne died in London on March 31, 1631. His bones lie somewhere within the grounds of St Paul's Cathedral.

Thomas Carew, a courtier and Cavalier poet (1594-1640), wrote Donne's elegy. In his poem he celebrates Donne's inventiveness and underlines how fresh an approach his must have been:

> The Muses' garden, with pedantic weeds
> O'erspread, was purged by thee, the lazy seeds
> Of servile imitation thrown away
> And fresh invention planted.

Carew's elegy was published with Donne's works in 1633 and ends with the fitting epitaph:

> Here lies a king that ruled as he thought fit
> The universal monarchy of wit.

The Metaphysical Poets

Meta means *after*, so metaphysical means after the physical. Metaphysics explores the nature of reality and the rational world, which is constantly being questioned. The Metaphysical Poets are therefore known for their ability to startle the reader and coax new perspective through paradoxical images, subtle argument, inventive syntax, and imagery from art, philosophy, and religion using an extended metaphor known as a conceit.

The term metaphysical, as applied to English and continental European poets of the seventeenth century, was used by Augustan poets John Dryden and Samuel Johnson to rebuke those poets for their 'unnaturalness.' As Goethe wrote, however, 'the unnatural, that too is natural,' and the metaphysical poets continue to be studied and revered for their intricacy and originality.

John Donne, along with similar but distinct poets such as George Herbert, Andrew Marvell, and Henry Vaughn, developed a poetic style in which philosophical and spiritual subjects were approached with reason and often concluded in paradox. This group of writers established meditation—based on the union of thought and feeling sought after in Jesuit Ignatian meditation— as a poetic mode.

Songs and Sonnets

None of John Donne's love poetry in *Songs and Sonnets* can be dated with any certainty because, although they were circulated in manuscripts during his lifetime, they were not published until two years after his death. The first edition, published in 1633, includes six songs, written to fit existing tunes, though the term sonnet is used loosely and should be interpreted to mean love lyrics. Most likely he wrote many of the poems in the 1590s, before he married Anne More in 1601, and then some of the more serious verses after his marriage. For all but one of the 'sonnets' (*Break of Day*) the reader can assume the narrator is a man, one who is frequently chasing pretty women, or trying to seduce them through wit and promises of pleasure; emanating from his 'Jack Donne' persona (later to become the widower Dr John Donne, Dean of St. Paul's).

The poetry in *Songs and Sonnets* usually mocks traditional images of love or uses extended metaphors called conceits. Some of the poems describe an exalted love that insists on and celebrates the body. A particular treatment of love can be found in the four 'Valedictory Poems' all of which Donne probably composed while married to Anne More. They dwell upon their separation during his travels and present love as intense and passionate. In *A Valediction: Forbidding Mourning* a conceit compares his love to a compass, the speaker reminds his absent beloved that the further they grow apart physically, the deeper and more expansive their love becomes spiritually.

Some poems treat love as a pleasure that does not last, where the speaker blames either himself or the woman. In *Woman's Constancy*, the narrator complains to his lover that she will undoubtedly leave him and is therefore guilty of 'falsehood,' only to call himself at the end of the poem a 'vain lunatic...for by tomorrow' he too will be ready to call it quits.

Several times we can imagine lovers either in bed or somewhere near it, as in *Break of Day* and *The Flea*; however, even though settings might be absent or vague, all of the poems have a distinct speaker and audience. Many begin with 'I' and his audience is quite frequently a woman whom he is wooing. For example, the poem *The Good-Morrow* begins, 'I wonder...what thou and I / Did till we loved.' In this poem, his purpose is to convince her that she is all he has ever dreamed of and hoped for, yet he also seeks sexual gratification, indicated by 'die,' a word which plays on a seventeenth-century pun that refers to orgasm.

Style

Donne sets words doggedly to the work of saying something, whether or no they step to the beat of the music. According to Ben Jonson, the contemporary playwright and friend, 'Donne, for not keeping of accent, deserved hanging'. And, of course, the way Donne meant his lines to be delivered is not always as beautiful as it is expressive. Often you'll find in his writing examples of what Samuel Johnson critically noted of 'metaphysical' poets, that their verses frequently '[stand] the trial of the finger better than of the ear.' He would thus be original at all costs, preferring himself to his art, and treated poetry as Æsop's master treated his slave, and broke what he could not bend.

Yet Donne's novelty of metre is only a part of his too deliberate novelty as a poet. His position in regard to the poetry of his time was that of a realistic writer, who makes a clean sweep of tradition, and puts everything down in the most modern words and with the help of the most trivial actual images, as in the first verse of *Love's Diet*:

> To what a cumbersome unwieldiness
> And burdenous corpulence my love had grown,
> But that I did, to make it less,
> And keep it in proportion,
> Give it a diet, made it feed upon
> That which love worst endures, discretion.

> Above one sigh a day I allow'd him not,
> Of which my fortune, and my faults had part;
> And if sometimes by stealth he got
> A she sigh from my mistress' heart,
> And thought to feast on that, I let him see
> 'Twas neither very sound, nor meant to me.

And when Donne writes of Love in *The Broken Heart* he declares:

> He swallows us and never chaws;
> By him, as by chain'd shot, whole ranks do die;
> He is the tyrant pike, our hearts the fry.

And, in his unwise insistence that every metaphor shall be absolutely new, he drags medical and alchemical and legal properties into verse full of personal passion, producing at times poetry which is a kind of disease of the intellect, a sick offshoot of science. Like most poets of powerful individuality, Donne lost precisely where he gained. That cumulative and crowding and sweeping intellect which builds up his greatest poems into miniature 'purges' too often the flowers as well as the weeds out of 'the Muses' garden.

Yet Donne's quality of passion is unique in English poetry. It is a rapture in which the mind is supreme, a reasonable rapture, and yet carried to a pitch of actual violence. The words mean things, and it is the things that matter. They can be brutal: 'For God's sake, hold your tongue, and let me love!' as if a long, pre-supposed self-repression gave way suddenly, in an outburst. 'Love, any devil else but you,' he begins, in his abrupt leap to the heart of the matter. Or else his exaltation will be grave, tranquil, measureless in assurance. Having something very minute and very exact to say, Donne also hates to leave anything out; dreading diffuseness, as he dreads the tame sweetness of an easy melody, he will use only the smallest possible number of words to render his thought; and so he is, on occasion, ingenious rather than always felicitous or harmonious.

Air and Angels

Twice or thrice had I lov'd thee,
Before I knew thy face or name;
So in a voice, so in a shapeless flame
Angels affect us oft, and worshipp'd be;
    Still when, to where thou wert, I came,
Some lovely glorious nothing I did see.
    But since my soul, whose child love is,
Takes limbs of flesh, and else could nothing do,
    More subtle than the parent is
Love must not be, but take a body too;
    And therefore what thou wert, and who,
        I bid Love ask, and now
That it assume thy body, I allow,
And fix itself in thy lip, eye, and brow.

Whilst thus to ballast love I thought,
And so more steadily to have gone,
With wares which would sink admiration,
I saw I had love's pinnace overfraught;
    Ev'ry thy hair for love to work upon
Is much too much, some fitter must be sought;
    For, nor in nothing, nor in things
Extreme, and scatt'ring bright, can love inhere;
    Then, as an angel, face, and wings
Of air, not pure as it, yet pure, doth wear,
    So thy love may be my love's sphere;
        Just such disparity
As is 'twixt air and angels' purity,
'Twixt women's love, and men's, will ever be.

Glossary

Ballast: material that is used to provide stability to a vessel
Overfraught: over filled
Pinnace: a rowing boat on a ship or small galleon.

Commentary

Air and Angels appears in *Songs and Sonnets,* in the second edition of John Donne's poems (1635). It is a challenging metaphysical poem that, within its elaborate verse form, explores the theme of love. A number of lines are ambiguous and therefore the poem remains, at least in part, open to interpretation. In the poem Donne compares the roles of a man and woman in a relationship to those of a powerful spiritual being and the matter it forms into a body. He uses ideas about angels familiar to the Elizabethans and at the end touches upon a difference which exists between men and women.

There are two sections or verses to the poem, each with its own separate theme and use of language. The first fourteen lines encapsulate the need for emotion to be placed in flesh and relies heavily on the use of 'earthly' terms such as 'limbs of flesh' and 'parent' as well as the fuller sense that the poet is attempting to 'ground' his thoughts to the mere earth-bound before launching into a discussion of higher things as the poem moves forward and branches out to include the metaphysical. The beginning of the poem is rather difficult to decipher, just as beauty is difficult to grasp and put into form.

At the beginning of the second set of fourteen lines, the poem still retains a beginning that is firmly rooted in the 'real' by invoking nautical terminology such as 'ballasts', 'sink' and 'pinnace' which at once puts the poem in an earth-bound context yet all the while is developing the idea that love cannot be attained through the physical alone. The images of heavy 'human' items such as the ballasts and boats are set against where love resides, which is somewhere between a 'thing' and 'nothing', somewhere where love is 'Extreme, and scattering bright'.

The poet therefore rejects the Platonic idea of love, love as something holy and spiritual, in the first verse, yet he is not content to simply worship physical beauty, which the Petrarchan poets did. He realizes the hollowness of the idealization of love, yet love needs an incarnation in which to manifest itself, otherwise, it remains invisible: 'Some lovely glorious nothing I did see'. The first attempt to find a suitable manifestation was the woman's body. She, as a physical being, must be the outward expression of his love. This suggests typical Elizabethan love poetry, in which every detail of the lady's body is listed as an object for admiration: 'thy lip, eye, brow'.

However, this proves inadequate so he switches his analogy to a boat or small galleon: 'love's pinnace'. His approach has loaded so much on to the woman's body (the vessel) that it has capsized. The physical manifestation must have been wrong. What, then, is the right medium? The answer is the woman's love itself. Just as air is not as pure as the angel it manifests, neither is the woman's love as pure as his, but it is the only way for it to show itself. This can, of course, be interpreted in several different ways – and Donne enjoys this ambiguous, paradoxical, possibly teasing, kind of ending. By the end of *Air and Angels* however, there seems to be a resolution to the question of such formlessness when the narrator decides: As is 'twixt air's and angels' purity, / Twixt women's love, and men's, will ever be' since here he concludes that love is just what he thought it was from the beginning - an idea without boundaries, much like air - formless and supernatural even though we may try to put it into the terms of flesh and reality. Therefore, by the end, the reader gets the sense that even though the speaker seems to have a notion of the power of love, he is not quite able to grasp it or give it the form and shape he seems to desire. One interpretation is that love simply cannot exist materially unless both a man and a woman are fully in love with each other i.e. a complete manifestation.

The mix between this world of the flesh and the world of the pure spirit of love are constantly playing off and one another as earthly and heavenly or supernatural images are juxtaposed. The form that a pure emotion like love takes is the central question and it posits the idea that beauty can never really be measured within the confines of the physical.

The poem therefore shows love taking on two forms, a shapeless and physical form, with love unable to exist in a vacuum. In the first verse there are illustrations and clear examples showing the two forms of love and the soul gives birth to love which has 'limbs of flesh.' This means love must also assume a physical form. John Donne than proceeds to say: 'That it assume thy body, I allow, / And fix, itself in thy lip, eye, and brow.' Yet mere admiration of her hair or some aspect of her beauty is not enough. There must be a substantial and objective expression of love.

It is one of the 'highly intellectualised' of Donne's love poems in which ideas of form and shapelessness are interwoven by language that is at once 'earthly' and heavenly. The title does not suggest the subject of love and he borrows images and concepts from metaphysics and navigation in order to prove the point that both physical base and mutuality are essential for the experience of love. That man's love is an angel and woman's love the air, and the harmony of the two is necessary for the concretization and consummation of love provides a sane and fitting conclusion to the poem, although this is only one possible interpretation.

The Anniversary

All kings, and all their favourites,
All glory of honours, beauties, wits,
The sun it self, which makes time, as they pass,
Is elder by a year now than it was
When thou and I first one another saw.
All other things to their destruction draw,
Only our love hath no decay;
This no to-morrow hath, nor yesterday;
Running it never runs from us away,
But truly keeps his first, last, everlasting day.

Two graves must hide thine and my corpse;
If one might, death were no divorce.
Alas! as well as other princes, we
—Who prince enough in one another be—

Must leave at last in death these eyes and ears,
Oft fed with true oaths, and with sweet salt tears;
But souls where nothing dwells but love
—All other thoughts being inmates—then shall prove
This or a love increasèd there above,
When bodies to their graves, souls from their graves remove.

And then we shall be throughly blest;
But now no more than all the rest.
Here upon earth we're kings, and none but we
Can be such kings, nor of such subjects be.
Who is so safe as we? where none can do
Treason to us, except one of us two.
True and false fears let us refrain,
Let us love nobly, and live, and add again
Years and years unto years, till we attain
To write threescore; this is the second of our reign.

Glossary

Two graves: implies they are not man and wife.
To write threescore: that the speaker hopes to celebrate sixty years.

Commentary

The Anniversary is among the most eloquent and accessible poems within the *Songs and Sonnets*. It is a quiet, celebratory poem, on the completion of the first year of a relationship and it is easy to link it to Donne's marriage to Anne More (1601), a marriage which, without consent, caused the poet a great deal of trouble. The celebratory, yet sometimes sombre language emphasises the royalty of love. In a way, this is an extension of the theme of the microcosm of the lovers' world, boldly proclaimed in *The Sun Rising*. If the lovers' world consists of only two inhabitants, then they are both royalty, the king and queen of their own little universe.

The other thing that anniversaries make us think of is the passing of time. Love and time were typically seen as enemies in Elizabethan poetry. There was a great fear of 'mutability', of the temporariness of things – and the word 'temporary' comes from the Latin word 'tempus', which means 'time'. Donne boldly defies this: their love is outside time. It has a timeless quality, unlike everything else from kings to the sun itself. 'Only our love hath no decay' is a typical Donne statement, drawing attention to the uniqueness of his experience of love. So, like heavenly time, it has no yesterday or tomorrow; it is eternally present.

However, death is a reality, and Donne does not flinch from thinking about it, since love and death might be seen as even greater enemies. Death is a leveler, though not so much in the conventional sense of everyone being brought down to the grave. In verse two he acknowledges this in passing, but goes on to stress the opposite: everyone being 'throughly blest'' by entering heavenly life, in that their souls will have been liberated from their bodies.

Death, therefore, does not threaten, but it is nothing to be celebrated, since in heaven their love will not be unique. So, at the end of the poem, he turns back to the unique present: let us live nobly, with no fear or jealousy, for the next sixty years. The final clause; 'this is the second of our reign' returns us confidently to the here and now.

In *The Anniversary* Donne's lover loves with his whole nature, and so collectedly because reason, in him, is not in conflict with passion, but passion's ally. His senses speak with unparalleled directness and the tone is an exemplary model of masculine sensual sobriety.

The Apparition

When by thy scorn, O murd'ress, I am dead
    And that thou think'st thee free
From all solicitation from me,
Then shall my ghost come to thy bed,
And thee, feign'd vestal, in worse arms shall see;
Then thy sick taper will begin to wink,
And he, whose thou art then, being tir'd before,
Will, if thou stir, or pinch to wake him, think
    Thou call'st for more,
And in false sleep will from thee shrink;
And then, poor aspen wretch, neglected thou
Bath'd in a cold quicksilver sweat wilt lie
    A verier ghost than I.
What I will say, I will not tell thee now,
Lest that preserve thee; and since my love is spent,
I'had rather thou shouldst painfully repent,
Than by my threat'nings rest still innocent.

Glossary

Feign'd vestal: a false virgin, or claiming to be saving her virginity as a Roman priestess of Vesta.
Taper: candle
Aspen: trembling, like the tree does in a breeze.
Quicksilver: semi-liquid mercury which resembles beads of sweat.
Verier ghost: even more ghost-like

Commentary

The Apparition, with its irregular structure and melodramatic rush of pure emotion, can be viewed as a disconcerting poem, but one worth unpicking. In the poem Donne incorporates a recurring theme in Petrarchan poetry: namely, the rejected lover's complaint. In the first line the narrator/rejected lover declares that he will die because his love is unrequited, murdered by the 'feign'd vestal'. He is as bitter as she is scornful of his soliciting and the poetic idea of dying for love is turned on its head. As a ghost he will haunt her when she thinks she is free and in the arms of a 'worse' lover. What is interesting is that he paints her as promiscuous, or at the very least a demanding lover with the man who fails to comfort her.

This revenge fantasy is 17 lines in length and written in varying meter and with an unusual rhyme scheme. The first four lines seem to set up a sonnet, abba, but then the fifth line is another b, followed by five lines cdcdc, then four lines, effe, are followed by a triplet, ggg. It can be seen as an ill-formed, extended or elongated Shakespearean sonnet, ending with the last three lines rhyming ggg, rather than the gg couplet.

The use of second person pronouns in the opening two lines, with thy and thou, subtly convey cold hostility and a lack of intimacy with the addressee. In the last four lines the speaker threatens his listener with a curse, something which he will not give her now; he would rather wait until she has sullied herself with other lovers. Then, when she has lost her innocence, something she might have retained if he speaks, she will have much in the future to 'painfully repent'.

The Apparition belongs to a series of hate poems in which Donne expresses a whole range of profound human feelings, some of which, according to one critic, have never been expressed, since Catullus, with such intolerable truth.

The Canonization

For God's sake hold your tongue, and let me love,
Or chide my palsy, or my gout,
My five gray hairs, or ruined fortune flout,
With wealth your state, your mind with arts improve,
Take you a course, get you a place,
Observe his honour, or his grace,
Or the king's real, or his stampèd face
Contemplate; what you will, approve,
So you will let me love.

Alas, alas, who's injured by my love?
What merchant's ships have my sighs drowned?
Who says my tears have overflowed his ground?
When did my colds a forward spring remove?
When did the heats which my veins fill
Add one more to the plaguy bill?
Soldiers find wars, and lawyers find out still
Litigious men, which quarrels move,
Though she and I do love.

Call us what you will, we are made such by love;
Call her one, me another fly,
We're tapers too, and at our own cost die,
And we in us find the eagle and the dove.
The phœnix riddle hath more wit
By us; we two being one, are it.
So, to one neutral thing both sexes fit.
We die and rise the same, and prove
Mysterious by this love.

We can die by it, if not live by love,
And if unfit for tombs and hearse
Our legend be, it will be fit for verse;
And if no piece of chronicle we prove,
We'll build in sonnets pretty rooms;
As well a well-wrought urn becomes
The greatest ashes, as half-acre tombs,
And by these hymns, all shall approve
Us canonized for Love.

And thus invoke us: 'You, whom reverend love
Made one another's hermitage;
You, to whom love was peace, that now is rage;
Who did the whole world's soul contract, and drove
Into the glasses of your eyes
(So made such mirrors, and such spies,
That they did all to you epitomize)

Countries, towns, courts: beg from above
A pattern of your love!'

Glossary

Chide my palsy: criticise my involuntary shakes (age related).
Plaguy bill: a list of deaths from the plague.

Commentary

The *Canonization* is an assertive monologue which opens with an imperative and a strong idiom. It concerns itself with the complexities of romantic love, was first published in 1633 and exemplifies Donne's sardonic wit and bold inventiveness. The title leads the reader to expect a poem concerned with saints and holy practices, but the very first line is a melodramatic demand which incorporates the idiomatic synecdoche: 'For God's sake hold your tongue'. The line appears almost blasphemous after such a title, yet by the end of the poem the reader is able to determine that the 'canonization' refers to the way that the poet's love will enter the canon of true love, becoming the pattern by which others judge their own love. *The Canonization* therefore suggests that the physical union of true lovers raises them to sainthood because the experience exceeds anything else offered on earth. Thus the mutual pleasure in physical union transforms love into a religious experience, transgressing the conventional moral attitudes of Donne's day. This conceit, involving saints and the pair of lovers, serves to emphasise the spirituality of the lovers' relationship.

    Like *The Ecstasy, The Canonization* presents a woman who mutually participates in love. This complicated poem, spoken ostensibly to someone who disapproves of the speaker's love affair, is written in the voice of a world-wise, sardonic courtier caught up in his feelings for a woman. The speaker asks his addressee to be quiet, and let him love.

    Most critics see the addressee as an unsympathetic male, one who, if he is to speak, is to criticize the narrator for other shortcomings (other than his tendency to love): his palsy, his gout, his 'five grey hairs,' or his ruined fortune. The listener is told to improve his mind or to 'get you a place' - for the purposes of self-aggrandizement, for which one must fawn upon the great. The listener is to become a sycophant, to reflect on the king's face (the 'stamp'd face' being a coin stamped with the king's likeness, thus to gaze upon money which implies the real object of the listener's desire). The theme here is plainly satirical, and it has sufficient sting to silence the listener, since the speaker is not obliged to order him to hold his tongue again. The things of the world can therefore be left to the addressee, leaving the speaker, in his dramatic monologue, to defend and later celebrate, with conceits and allusions, his transcendent love.

Yet the speaker takes the opportunity to develop the satire in verse two: the love of power, the love of wealth, the love of military or judicial conquest - this, he implies, is the kind of love abroad in this world. Through the use of five interrogatives he challenges the listener, who now becomes increasing disembodied. Nobody, the argument runs, is hurt by their love. They are not sinking ships, causing floods, delaying spring, spreading diseases or supporting wars or lawsuits. Here Donne references conventional Petrarchan metaphors of courtly love (love-poems were full of claims like 'My tears are rain, my sighs storms' and were poetic clichés by that time). He concludes that argumentative soldiers and lawyers can still bicker even though he finds contentment in love. Soldiers still find wars and lawyers still find litigious men, regardless of the emotions of the speaker and his lover. The irony is heavy here, where the harmless repertoire of the lover - sighs and tears and colds and heats and so on - is sarcastically played off against the realities of a vulgar, mean and exploitative world.

By the end of the second verse the speaker has effectively belittled the world that had censured him for his romantic loving, and so has opened up the potential for a full ironic subversion, which he achieves in verse three with a particularly clever manoeuvre. It is both bold and witty, because the argument here turns essentially on the popular

Renaissance pun on the word 'die', which carried the sense of 'orgasm'. Because the lovers 'rise' again after they 'die', the speaker claims, they endure beyond their own death, and so there is something mysterious, perhaps miraculous, about them, and this can be taken as a sign of sanctification: therefore, they are saints of love, and are canonized as such.

In the third verse the speaker tells his addressee to 'Call us what you will' and employs metaphors that will help explain the intensity and uniqueness of his love. First, he says that the addressee can 'Call her one, me another fly', then, like candles, they will burn out on their own, yet are reborn together in fire like the fabled Phoenix. They may destroy themselves in the act of burning with passion for one another, yet by the middle of the poem, Donne translates their love to a higher plane. The speaker compares himself and his beloved to the eagle and dove, a reference to the Renaissance idea in which the eagle flies in the sky above the earth while the dove transcends the skies to reach heaven. He immediately shifts to the image of the Phoenix, another death-by-fire symbol (the Phoenix is a bird that repeatedly burns in fire and comes back to life out of the ashes), suggesting that even though their flames of passion will consume them, the speaker and his beloved will be reborn from the ashes of their love.

In their resurrection, their relationship has become a paradox. The key paradox of love is that two individuals become one. By uniting in this way, they 'prove/Mysterious by this love'. The new union is unsexed even though it incorporates both sexes: 'to one neutral thing both sexes fit,' as in Christ there is no longer any male or female (Galatians 3:28) or as in Plato's Symposium where the original human beings had the marks of both sexes before they were split into male and female, each person being left to seek his or her other half.

In the fourth verse the speaker explores the possibility of canonization in verse, thus opening out to consider the legacy of the poet's love with his beloved. Their love will endure in legend; the language of 'verse' and 'chronicle' suggests canonization at nearly the level of Scripture. Even if their love is not quite at that level, songs will be sung and sonnets composed commemorating their romance. Their love is self-contained and perfect, like a 'well-wrought urn' yet the ashes in this urn are meant to spread, in this case covering half an acre; symbolic of spreading the tale of perfect love throughout the world.

In the final verse he explores his and his lover's roles as the saints of love, to whom generations of future lovers will appeal for help. It therefore voices the speaker's sense of future vindication over the critic. The speaker expects that the rest of the world will 'invoke' himself and his beloved, similar to the way Catholics invoke saints in their prayers. In this vision of the future, the lovers' legend has grown, and they have reached a kind of sainthood; thereby equating worldly human love with the ascetic life of unworldly saints. They are role models for the rest of the world, as 'Countries, towns, courts beg from above/A pattern of your love' From the lovers' perspective, the whole world is present as they look into each other's eyes. Therefore, even if the love affair is impossible in the real world, it can become legendary through poetry, and the speaker and his lover will be like saints to later generations of lovers. (Hence the title, *The Canonization*, refers to the process by which people are inducted into the canon of saints).

The Canonization is deservedly one of Donne's most famous and most written-about poems. Some critics argue that the poem is what it seems to be, an anti-political love poem, while biographical critics see it as being based on the events in Donne's life at the time of the poem's composition. Whether it is Donne reflecting on the 'ruined fortune' and dashed political hopes is largely a matter of personal temperament, yet it is probably best to understand the poem as the sort of droll, passionate speech-act it is, a highly sophisticated defense of love against the corrupting values of politics and privilege.

The argument in the poem is forceful, suggestive and witty and, as the argument develops, the lovers become love's martyrs, and therefore saints. The term 'canonized' is used in the religious sense but also mischievously - by implying that he and his lover will be elevated to the level of saints because they love as they do. The speaker uses colloquial words, rough idioms and a speech-like rhythm. He asks rhetorical questions, employs idioms, references common metaphors and, in tone, is frequently rough and conversational, some might say his argument is perfectly balanced between a kind of sophisticated sensibility and passionate amorous abandon.

      The poem consists of five nine-line verses, each verse an argument set forth, as though in a five act play, to demonstrate the purity and power of the speaker's love. The lines are metered in iambic lines ranging from trimeter to pentameter; in each of the nine-line verses, the first, third, fourth, and seventh lines are in pentameter, the second, fifth, sixth, and eighth in tetrameter, and the ninth in trimeter. The rhyme scheme in each verse is abbaccaa and each verse fittingly ends with the word 'love'.

The Flea

Mark but this flea, and mark in this,
How little that which thou deniest me is ;
It suck'd me first, and now sucks thee,
And in this flea our two bloods mingled be.
Thou know'st that this cannot be said
A sin, nor shame, nor loss of maidenhead;
Yet this enjoys before it woo,
And pamper'd swells with one blood made of two;
And this, alas ! is more than we would do.

O stay, three lives in one flea spare,
Where we almost, yea, more than married are.
This flea is you and I, and this
Our marriage bed, and marriage temple is.
Though parents grudge, and you, we're met,
And cloister'd in these living walls of jet.
Though use make you apt to kill me,
Let not to that self-murder added be,

And sacrilege, three sins in killing three.

Cruel and sudden, hast thou since
Purpled thy nail in blood of innocence?
Wherein could this flea guilty be,
Except in that drop which it suck'd from thee?
Yet thou triumph'st, and say'st that thou
Find'st not thyself nor me the weaker now.
'Tis true ; then learn how false fears be ;
Just so much honour, when thou yield'st to me,
Will waste, as this flea's death took life from thee.

Glossary

Cloister'd: a covered walk in a religious building. The flea represents the temple in which their marriage has taken place.

Commentary

The Flea is an erotic metaphysical poem (published in 1633) that uses the conceit of a flea, which has sucked blood from the male speaker and his female lover, to serve as an extended metaphor (or conceit) for the relationship between them. The speaker tries to convince a lady to sleep with him, arguing that if their blood mingling in the flea is innocent, then sexual mingling would also be innocent. His argument hinges on the belief that blood mixes during sexual intercourse. *The Flea* belongs, surprisingly, to a long list of sixteenth-century love poems and paintings and the use of a flea in an erotically charged context goes back at least as far as Ovid.

In Donne's poem, as with many other Metaphysical works, a certain amount of the dramatic context is given, but the main force of the poem lies in the persuasive skill of the poet to move the lady to making love with him by using outrageous analogies. In his persuasion, he uses philosophic and theological conceits and Donne is able to hint at the erotic without explicitly referring to sex by using images such as the flea that 'pamper'd swells with the blood of the lady. This evokes the idea of an erection. The speaker complains that This is more than we would do!'.

The speaker later claims it would be 'sacrilege' to kill the flea. He holds the flea up in the second stanza as 'our marriage bed' and 'our marriage temple,' begging for the lady to spare its innocent life. He argues that by killing the flea, she would be killing herself, himself, and the flea itself, 'Three crimes in killing three'. The lady, in the third stanza, kills the flea, presumably rejecting the speaker's advances. He then claims she will lose no more honour when she decides to sleep with him than she did when she killed the flea.

Fleas, of course, were a common feature of life in the early modern period, especially when bedding was rarely changed, yet Donne manages to use the more unpleasant aspect of the flea's bloodsucking to his advantage. In the first of the three verses, he merely uses the flea as an analogy for a purely physical union. The conceit is that the flea has united their blood by biting both of them. Ironically, this is more union than the poet feels is likely to happen between him and his lady friend.

In the second verse she is going to squash the flea. The speaker urges her to spare it, using theological arguments. The 'three lives in one' of the flea (her blood, his and its) is a clear reference to the Christian idea of the Trinity. The flea is seen as their marriage 'temple', which it would be 'sacrilege' to destroy. The idea of a physical body being a temple appears in the New Testament (1 Corinthians 3:17). 'Sacrilege' is where something seen as holy in a religion is destroyed. So if she were to kill the flea, she would be killing him (an example of synecdoche, since the flea has a drop of the poet's blood, which then symbolises him altogether); she would be committing suicide, and she would be committing sacrilege. There is also the Christian teaching that any sexual union is a making into 'one flesh' (Corinthians).

The addressee rejects his argument and when it's done thinks she has outwitted the poet. But then the argument takes an entirely different and contradictory turn - the death of the flea, which contains both their blood, hasn't made either of them any the weaker; by extension having sex would not damage her honour any more than the death of the flea damages their well being. If squashing the flea is such a slight thing, he argues by analogy, then any loss of honour is about as insignificant as the flea's death. And so the speaker tries to break down the woman's resistance with a clever and highly entertaining bit of poetic logic.

At first glance, it is the image of the flea that leaps out at the reader, but closer scrutiny reveals a sexual current with 'sucks', 'swells', 'pamper'd', 'blood' and 'maidenhead'. This apparently innocuous discussion of a fleabite is really another discourse in favour of sex. The seriousness and outrageousness of the argument is further emphasised by the cluster of words to do with religion: 'sin', 'sacrilege', 'guilt', 'cloister'd', 'innocence', 'temple' and the echoes of the Holy Trinity in the description of the 'three' - the narrator, the woman and the flea. Such lexical groupings seem so out of place in a poem as earth-bound and trivial as this yet by humorously couching sexual desire in religious terms it attempts to break down the woman's defences. When you add to this the legal lexis of 'confession', 'injury', 'death' and 'self-murder', the emotional pressure on the woman is even greater.

From the very first word of the poem imperatives appear: 'Mark', 'Confess', 'stay', 'let not', 'learn'. All are forceful demands from a speaker who wants the woman to do as he says. Interestingly, the final imperative 'learn' takes us to the heart of the narrator's supposed purpose, which is to use argument to change the woman's thinking, to teach her a different way of thinking about sex. The imperative at the beginning of the second verse is used with the exclamation 'Oh'. This both suggests the spoken voice, drawing the reader into the very private space in which the poem takes place and emphasises the mock-heroic drama of the moment, with the poet trying to prevent the woman from killing the flea, as if a murder is about to take place.

Compound sentences are also used to powerful effect, perhaps pulling together the threads of the argument to make them clear. Lines like 'This flea is you and I, and this/Our marriage bed, and marriage temple is.' uses a compound sentence to draw out very simply the analogy between the flea and their relationship. In the first and second verses it is only in the final triplet that the words 'Yet' and 'Though' introduce a qualification that signals a shift in thought.

Interestingly, the events within the poem are implied rather than stated, with the reader filling in the gaps. 'Oh stay' tells us that the woman is about to kill the flea and 'Cruel and sudden, hast thou since/Purpled thy nail' tells us that the flea has been killed, but at no point does the speaker actually tell us this sequence of events. It's like a one-sided conversation, where we imagine the other side of what is happening.

Furthermore, the conversational register of an intimate tête a tête is emphasised in the line 'Where we almost, yea more than married are', where the interrupted construction has the quality of unscripted speech. Putting the formal and informal together in this way contributes to the humour, with basic desires being elevated using formal, high-flown and exaggerated language. This style is sometimes called the 'mock-heroic', with grand language being used to comic effect.

As well as shifting between a legalistic formality and an intimate conversational voice numerous oppositions appear within the poem. However, many of these, by the end, are shown not to be true oppositions - the idea of virginity equating with honour and good reputation and not being a virgin equating with loss of honour is rejected. The climax of the argument is in the last two lines of the poem, where the rhyme on 'me' and 'thee' emphasises the way in which the poem has been structured around this particular opposition, between the man and woman.

In structure the poem alternates metrically between lines in iambic tetrameter and lines in iambic pentameter, a 4-5 stress pattern ending with two pentameter lines at the end of each verse. The rhyme scheme in each verse is similarly regular, in couplets, though it ends with a triple rhyme: aabbccddd.

As with many of his poems, Donne's poise of hinting at the erotic without ever explicitly referring to sex, while at the same time leaving no doubt as to exactly what he means, is as much a source of the poem's worth as the conceit he employs.

The Good-Morrow

I wonder by my troth, what thou and I
Did, till we loved? Were we not wean'd till then?
But suck'd on country pleasures, childishly?
Or snorted we in the Seven Sleepers' den?
'Twas so; but this, all pleasures fancies be;
If ever any beauty I did see,
Which I desired, and got, 'twas but a dream of thee.

And now good-morrow to our waking souls,
Which watch not one another out of fear;
For love all love of other sights controls,
And makes one little room an everywhere.
Let sea-discoverers to new worlds have gone;
Let maps to other, worlds on worlds have shown;
Let us possess one world; each hath one, and is one.

My face in thine eye, thine in mine appears,
And true plain hearts do in the faces rest;
Where can we find two better hemispheres
Without sharp north, without declining west?
Whatever dies, was not mix'd equally;
If our two loves be one, or thou and I
Love so alike that none can slacken, none can die.

Glossary

The Seven Sleepers: hid inside a cave outside the city of Ephesus around 250 AD to escape a persecution. Having fallen

asleep they awoke 180 years later and were seen by the people of the now-Christian city before dying.
Good morrow: an early modern 'good morning' greeting.
Sharp north: a cold region in the north.
Declining west: no sun setting, often meaning death.

Commentary

The Good-morrow appeared in *Songs and Sonnets* in the original 1633 edition and, like *The Sun Rising*, is one of Donne's love songs, celebrating the joys of a completely unified love. The idea it posits is if the lovers are unchanging in their love then they will achieve immortality, since only what changes, dies. The two lovers therefore make up a complete world which is self-sufficient and self-absorbing.

In the opening line the first person pronoun, 'I', leaps out, asks a question and demands an answer, even though the question posed is a semi-rhetorical, while the other person is never allowed a second to reply. In the first verse the narrator is talking to his partner and looks back to when they were not in love. Four interrogatives are employed in quick succession conveying the idea that they were children. Whatever pleasures they experienced were mere unrealities ('fancies') compared to what they have now. Any beauty (possibly any female beauty) was a mere dream or steppingstone leading to or to be set against the present reality. The opening verse contains several interesting images with babies being weaned, suggesting the immaturity of their previous emotional life, and the 'Seven Sleepers'.

The second verse reflects on the current situation and begins with a note of restrained triumph. There are no questions any more and the verse finishes with a persuasive plea for them to enjoy their world. This suggests that the lovers have woken now into a reality shaped by love. The room where they are in bed is their world, and nothing exists outside its walls. The compound noun 'sea-discovers' introduces the idea of worlds elsewhere, but this merely foregrounds the need for them to possess their own private world.

In the third verse one complete world suggests that each is a hemisphere perfectly complementing the other. The poet concludes by suggesting that if they can stay totally constant as lovers, then they cannot die, since, according to early modern thinking, only what is contrary or of different measure can disintegrate. A perfect harmony, symbolized by the globe, will be theirs. Yet the poem seems to end on a note of some doubt: 'If ... or ... '. Perhaps, after all, Donne cannot any longer sustain the idea of their immortal love in their new world created being invulnerable.

As is usual with a Donne poem, the argument in *The Good-morrow* is carried on through the images or conceits used. Here we have the lovers waking to a new 'immortal' life in a new world, both conceits created by their mutual love. Their new life is to be one without fear in keeping with the idea in the Bible that 'Perfect love casts out fear' (John).

With regard to form, each verse is regular, consisting of seven lines and rhyming ababccc. The c-rhyme is today a little weak at times: 'gone', 'shown', 'one' are more half or eye rhymes than sound ones. English pronunciation has changed somewhat since Donne's day, so that a final '-ly' did actually rhyme with 'I'. All the lines have ten syllables (pentameters) except for the last lines in each verse, which have twelve (alexandrine). As with other poems, Donne frequently avoids any smoothly flowing rhythm: the 'I' voice, for example, is too intrusive to allow that. Even though a line like: 'Let maps to other, worlds on worlds have shown;' is technically an iambic pentameter, the number of monosyllabic words and the consonant clusters make it a ungainly line to read, but that is deliberate: the world outside is an awkward and ungainly place, in contrast to their perfect world.

Woman's Constancy

Now thou has loved me one whole day,
Tomorrow when you leav'st, what wilt thou say?
Wilt thou then antedate some new-made vow?
    Or say that now
We are not just those persons which we were?
Or, that oaths made in reverential fear
Of Love, and his wrath, any may forswear?
Or, as true deaths true marriages untie,
So lovers' contracts, images of those,
Bind but till sleep, death's image, them unloose?
    Or, your own end to justify,
For having purposed change and falsehood, you
Can have no way but falsehood to be true?
Vain lunatic, against these 'scapes I could
    Dispute and conquer, if I would,
    Which I abstain to do,
For by tomorrow, I may think so too.

Commentary

Woman's Constancy is a 17-line lyric poem on matters of love and was circulated, in various versions, before it was printed in 1633 (having been probably been written before 1600). In the poem the narrator addresses a woman with whom he is about to spend the night. The speaker believes that the woman will want to leave him in the morning and argues with her by suggesting the excuses that she will use when she tries to leave. The speaker's argument, which is full of interrogatives, frames a response yet chooses not to refute the opposing argument for fear he will feel the same in the morning.

    The first technique that the speaker employs is to present the woman's arguments in a derisive way. The speaker is able to do this since he delivers the arguments of the woman. The speaker's opening line sets up a sarcastic tone for the poem by suggesting that the woman thinks 'one whole day' is a significant period of time. This tone carries over to when he presents the woman's possible excuses and makes them sound absurd. He asks whether she will 'antedate' (or backdate) a vow made to a new lover, or whether she will claim that she and the speaker are not the same persons they once were, so that she no longer has any obligations to him. The speaker's use of questions also disparages the woman's argument, since a tone of disbelief accompanies each question. 'Woman's Constancy' is unique amongst Donne's poems in that the counterargument gets the majority of lines. Since the speaker disdainfully frames the arguments, however, he is in control and the reader is never swayed by any of the excuses the woman could make.

Yet in turning to the excuses themselves, some of them are strong and would make valid counterarguments for the woman if she were to use them. Two possible excuses in particular are logical and one is based on contract law. Contracts are considered binding, unless an exception clause is met. The focus on arguing a contract is to prove the exception has occurred. In the first excuse, the speaker claims that the lovers' contract can be invalidated since it was made in fear of Love's wrath. A common aspect of any contract is that it is not binding if it was signed out of fear. The woman's excuse, therefore, seems valid since she shows that she has met the exception.

In the second excuse, an agreement to spend the night is likened to an imitation of marriage. If marriages are no longer binding at death, then sleep, which is like death, should end the lovers' contract. This excuse is sound since she would make her argument in the morning when sleep would have occurred so the exception would be met. Will she try to claim, he wonders, that in order to be true to herself she must be false to him? In looking at the language of the excuses and leaving out the condescending way the speaker delivers them, the excuses are persuasive since they are logically sound.

The speaker's control is then reflected in the poem's amusing conclusion when he suggests the possibility of using the excuses himself in the morning. After labelling her a 'Vain lunatic' he explains that he could challenge every argument and win any debate if he wanted to do so. However, he proclaims that he chooses not to, because tomorrow he may feel as she does. Regardless of whether he cares or not, the control and indifference he shows by not refuting the excuses cause him to win anyway.

      Stylistically, this poem is typical of Donne's writings in that it is a dramatic monologue (since it presents only one person's point of view) it deals with love or problems in love, and it is witty. The speed with which the speaker's mind imagines new arguments and anticipates and preempts a response demonstrates Donne's inventiveness. The speaker is cynical, and irony is a major feature of this poem. The wit of the poem makes it humorous, dealing, as it does, with the fickleness or mutability of a secular and ephemeral kind of love.

To His Mistress Going to Bed

Come, madam, come, all rest my powers defy,
Until I labour, I in labour lie.
The foe oft-times having the foe in sight,
Is tired with standing though he never fight.
Off with that girdle, like heaven's zone glistering,
But a far fairer world encompassing.
Unpin that spangled breastplate which you wear,
That th'eyes of busy fools may be stopped there.
Unlace yourself, for that harmonious chime
Tells me from you that now it is bed time.
Off with that happy busk, which I envy,
That still can be, and still can stand so nigh.
Your gown going off, such beauteous state reveals,
As when from flowery meads th'hills shadow steals.
Off with your wiry coronet and show
The hairy diadem which on you doth grow:
Now off with those shoes: and then safely tread
In this love's hallowed temple, this soft bed.
In such white robes heaven's angels used to be

Received by men; thou, Angel, bring'st with thee
A heaven like Mahomet's Paradise; and though
Ill spirits walk in white, we easily know
By this these Angels from an evil sprite:
Those set our hairs, but these our flesh upright.
 License my roving hands, and let them go
Before, behind, between, above, below.
O my America! my new-found-land,
My kingdom, safeliest when with one man manned,
My mine of precious stones, my empery,
How blest am I in this discovering thee!
To enter in these bonds is to be free;
Then where my hand is set, my seal shall be.
 Full nakedness! All joys are due to thee,
As souls unbodied, bodies unclothed must be,
To taste whole joys. Gems which you women use
Are as Atlanta's balls, cast in men's views,
That when a fool's eye lighteth on a gem,
His earthly soul may covet theirs, not them:
Like pictures, or like books' gay coverings made
For lay-men, are all women thus arrayed.
Themselves are mystic books, which only we
(Whom their imputed grace will dignify)
Must see revealed. Then, since that I may know,
As liberally as to a midwife, show
Thyself: cast all, yea, this white linen hence,
There is no penance due to innocence:
 To teach thee, I am naked first; why than,
What need'st thou have more covering than a man?

Glossary

Atlanta's balls: a reference to Ovid's story in which Atlanta would only marry a man who could beat her in a race. Hippomenes distracts her by throwing three golden balls down in front of her and therefore wins the race.
Busk: the rigid element of a corset placed at the centre front. The corsets worn between the fifteenth and eighteenth

centuries had busks that were intended to keep the front of the corset straight and upright. They were made of wood, ivory, or bone slipped into a pocket and tied in place with a lace called the busk point. These busks were often carved and decorated, or inscribed with messages, and were popular gifts from men to their sweethearts.

Imputed grace: a reference to Calvin's theology that only a few are chosen for salvation.

Neoplatonism: a philosophic system based on Platonic doctrine and Oriental mysticism to which Christian influences were later added. It holds that all existence emanates from a single source to which souls can be reunited.

Spangled Breastplate: the decorated front piece of the dress, covering the breast and the pit of the stomach.

Commentary

Elegy XIX: To His Mistress Going to Bed mocks the solemn Petrarchan poems of the day which frequently focused on the despair and heartache brought about by unattainable love. However, because of its energetic, bawdy wit and its explicit portrayal of erotic desire it wasn't printed until 1654 and didn't appear in Donne's *Poems* until 1669.

In the poem the speaker urges his mistress into bed. Donne's speaker fervently describes undressing and caressing his mistress, and at the end, the narrator reveals that he is fully unclothed and erect. The process of disrobing is followed from top to toe, centred on the belly and vulva, and each stage compares the beauty of dress as external decoration with the natural beauty of the undressed woman.

Donne's elegy was influenced by Ovid's 'Elegies', in which Ovid used wit and detachment in describing the male lover's aggressive pursuit of women. By combining Petrarch's technique of wooing from afar with Ovid's sexually aggressive language and style, Donne creates a parody of the conventional love sonnet, and an early specimen of libertine poetry. Several poetic conventions, such as the blazon, metaphysical conceit, neoplatonism and allusion are also used in this work.

Ironically, Donne's speaker uses a blazon, or a record of virtues and excellencies, to describe his mistress undressing (lines 5–18). While standard Petrarchan blazons were used to list a woman's honourable attributes, such as her beauty or chasteness, Donne's poem removes the woman from the pedestal on which she had been adored and places an erotic emphasis on an otherwise virtuous list. Instead of speaking of his mistress's virtues, Donne's speaker focuses solely on her appearance and his response to her undressing.

The poem is also peppered with metaphorical allusions. In line 21 Donne refers to 'Mahomet's Paradise', which was rumoured to be peopled with beautiful women ready to satisfy the carnal desires of the male inhabitants. Similarly, Donne mentions that 'Gems which you women use/Are like Atlanta's balls, cast in men's views' (35–6); in Greek mythology Atlanta rejected all suitors who could not defeat her in a race; Hippomenes eventually defeated her by dropping three apples or golden balls along the race trail, which Atlanta stopped to pick up. Donne's use of religious allusions and eroticism suggests that the poet sees physical love or the appreciation of the female body as something divine.

Furthermore, the erotic imagery complements Donne's mimicking of Ovidian wit. In the blazon, Donne's speaker orders: 'Off with that happy busk, which I envy'; Donne's speaker uses the busk as an allusion to the phallus, although it is unclear whether or not the speaker envies the busk because of its proportions, or because it is close to the mistress's body. The narrator asks his mistress to 'Show/The hairy diadem which on you doth grow' or let her hair down, which creates, particularly for the early modern reader, an image of female sexual liberty within the bedroom setting (it is also used later in Thomas Carew's *A Rapture*).

And then Donne's metaphysical conceit occurs in line 27; 'O my America! my new-found-land / My kingdom, safeliest when with one man man'd / My mine of precious stones, My empery/How blest am I in this discovering thee!'. K. W. Gransden sees this excerpt as an 'analogy from

Elizabethan navigation and discovery, by which means he [the speaker] depicts the lover's journey to consummation in the most modern possible fashion. Donne neatly hits the traditional estimate of love by expressing it in terms of an adventure'. Here, Gransden commends Donne's comparison of sexual intercourse to an adventure, which was a modern way for his speaker to coax the mistress into bed. Donne's metaphysical conceit also dabbles in gendered power dynamics of early modern England. Dr Ilona Bell suggests that 'If the woman is [the speaker's] kingdom and his empire, he is her king and emperor, revelling unabashedly in his masculine dominion over her', which suggests that Donne's speaker takes a position of superiority and governance over his mistress. However, it is important to note that without the 'new-found-land', or the mistress, Donne's speaker would not be king. As much as the mistress needs the speaker, the speaker needs the mistress. This is also relevant in the last lines of the poem: 'To teach thee, I am naked first, why then/What needst thou have more covering then a man?'; Donne's speaker removes his clothes to guide, or teach, his mistress; however, since he is naked first, he places himself in a place of vulnerability. Bell notes that 'male domination [was] fundamental to Donne's poetic and cultural inheritance. Not surprisingly, therefore, Donne's poems acknowledge the sexual stereotypes and gender hierarchy that subordinated early modern women to men; however, his poems also dramatise the ways in which Donne challenged... the patriarchal polity and society into which [he was] born and died'. Bell's theory is thus supported by supplying the reader with a metaphysical conceit that places the speaker over his mistress, but in a way that obviously shows his dependence on her, as well as providing an open-ended scenario where the man is either guiding his mistress into nudity or left vulnerable as she remains clothed.

  Although the elegy is not Donne's most credible neoplatonic work, there is one instance where transcendent love is mentioned. Donne's speaker mentions that 'As souls unbodied, bodies uncloth'd must be', which suggests that the spiritual connection of two souls outside of the body, or a neoplatonic love, is just as crucial and necessary to a relationship as physical, erotic love.

A Jet Ring Sent

Thou art not so black as my heart,
Nor half so brittle as her heart, thou art;
What would'st thou say? Shall both our properties by thee be spoke,
Nothing more endless, nothing sooner broke?

Marriage rings are not of this stuff;
Oh, why should ought less precious, or less tough
Figure our loves? except in thy name thou have bid it say,
'I am cheap, and nought but fashion; fling me away.'

Yet stay with me since thou art come,
Circle this finger's top, which didst her thumb;
Be justly proud, and gladly safe, that thou dost dwell with me;
She that, O, broke her faith, would soon break thee.

Commentary

The lady has returned to the speaker a jet ring that he once gave to her as a token of their love. Its casual language poignantly conveys a wistful expression of pain, resignation, and tenderness as the rejected lover speaks, in meditation, to and for an inanimate object. The cheap love token symbolizes the fragility of his failed love affair and Donne throws his despairing voice into the ring: 'I am cheap, and nought but fashion, throw me away'.

As within many of Donne's poems the speaker makes and unmakes arguments, though within *A Jet Ring Sent* the focus is clear, as is the language. The words used are mostly monosyllabic with the poet, by packing consonants into each line, giving most lines a brittle sound. The metre generally is iambic, though the unusually long third line in each verse contains 14 syllables (a 'fourteener'). Donne uses various line lengths to great effect, but the fourteener is unusual for him. What is more, in the first two verses this line is punctuated with a strong caesura after a rhetorical question, which breaks down the iambic rhythm even further. The overall effect sounds very much like casual speech, which is part of the poem's charm.

Jet is a minor black gemstone (the eponymous 'jet black'), but is not strictly a mineral: like coal, it originates in decaying wood fossilized under extreme pressure. It is relatively soft, warmer to the touch than rock or glass. In the early modern period jet was often used for trinkets, such as rings (though not for a wedding), and these were sometimes reinforced with silver, and engraved with a posy.

At the beginning of the poem, the ring still symbolizes the fragile union between two lovers: it is black, almost as dark as his heart, and it is brittle, or changeable, like her heart; 'nothing [is] more endless' than his love; 'nothing [is] sooner broke' than her vows. The dramatic posture of the speaker with his black (bitter, melancholy) heart gives way to a complete focus on the ring. Donne personifies the ring and dramatizes a conversation with it, asking it questions ('what would'st thou say?') and completing the ring's replies, first indirectly ('speaking' both lovers' properties), then, in the second verse, directly. Note how the ring's imagined reply sounds just like the speaker: casual, quiet, matter-of-fact. If the ring cannot figure a more perfect love, the fault lies with the speaker himself for giving his lady a ring of jet. The very name insinuates to the wearer what she should do with it: 'fling me away,' punning on the French jette, jetter (to throw). 'I'm cheap, and naught but fashion; fling me away'. Yet now that the ring has returned to the speaker, he refuses to throw it away. He tries it on and briefly considers his lady's impossibly small hands ('circle this finger's top that didst her thumb': a ring she wore on her thumb barely fits the top of his finger). He vows to keep his tiny companion safe – safer than it ever could be with the unfaithful woman. The jet ring, cheap and fickle as it is, thus reinforces for the speaker the value of keeping one's faith. It also allows him to externalize his self-pity as a gesture of care.

The jet ring, employed as a metaphysical conceit, is examined through multiple discrete qualities, each with its own significance: blackness, brittleness, circularity, smallness. Donne's meditation on the jet ring fashions a 'less precious' and 'less tough' material into an emblem of love and loss, but what is more, by the end of the poem Donne has constructed a metaphor of a broken promise that contains a narrative of its own creation. Thus by possessing the ring the speaker conveys an act of exposure and it grants him an interpretive power and freedom he otherwise would lack.

The Relic

When my grave is broke up again
    Some second guest to entertain,
    (For graves have learn'd that woman head,
    To be to more than one a bed)
        And he that digs it, spies
A bracelet of bright hair about the bone,
        Will he not let' us alone,
And think that there a loving couple lies,
Who thought that this device might be some way
To make their souls, at the last busy day,
Meet at this grave, and make a little stay?

    If this fall in a time, or land,
    Where mis-devotion doth command,
    Then he, that digs us up, will bring
    Us to the bishop, and the king,
        To make us relics; then
Thou shalt be a Mary Magdalen, and I
        A something else thereby;
All women shall adore us, and some men;
And since at such time miracles are sought,
I would have that age by this paper taught

What miracles we harmless lovers wrought.

> First, we lov'd well and faithfully,
> Yet knew not what we lov'd, nor why;
> Difference of sex no more we knew
> Than our guardian angels do;
>   Coming and going, we
> Perchance might kiss, but not between those meals;
>   Our hands ne'er touch'd the seals
> Which nature, injur'd by late law, sets free;
> These miracles we did, but now alas,
> All measure, and all language, I should pass,
> Should I tell what a miracle she was.

Glossary

Woman-head: or womanhood, or suggesting women were promiscuous or also cared for their baby in bed.
Busy day: Day of Judgment when countless people will be resurrected.
Mis-devotion: it was against the doctrine of the Anglican Church to invoke saints.
Seals: there was no sexual contact.
Late law: society's conventions on propriety in sexual matters.

Commentary

The Relic is an early work, another poem gathered into the posthumously published *Songs and Sonnets*. It is clearly a 'song' and, with the rhythmic ebb and flow of a madrigal, moving lightly between four, three and five-beat lines in each verse, it only has to be muttered softly aloud for the melody to emerge.
        The language is relatively simple and the tone is loving, yet it is a franker and more sensual poem, and there's the knowingness of the sexually experienced young man-about town. However, unlike many of his poems, *The Relic* is a Petrarchan tribute, and was probably addressed to Mrs

Magdalen Herbert, an aristocratic, pious and virtuous married woman who would have accepted the compliment in the spirit in which it was given.

There is a playful tone in many lines; and it is not to be taken too seriously. The poem systematically argues that their love equates to that of saints yet the closing verse is a sober justification of their love because it is harmless and platonic – non-sexual and therefore pure and miraculous.

Donne begins the poem with an image of the speaker's exhumation. In the Elizabethan period graves were not as neatly arranged as they are today, and it was common for graves to be dug up to receive a second or third corpse (for example, in *Hamlet* Ophelia is buried in a grave that contains the bones of Yorick, the king's jester). Like a grave in the 17th century, 'woman-head' (womanhood) is 'to more than one a bed'. This is an ambiguous line which might suggest that women are sexually promiscuous (which the woman eulogised isn't) or that their bodies have a dual role, being shared by the male lover and the children of the union. It is even possible to imagine a reference to a child in the womb.

In the first verse a light-heartedness prevails in the four four-beat lines and the following foreshortened trimeter, 'And he that digs it, spies'. And then comes that haunting line of iambic pentameter: 'A bracelet of bright hair about the bone.' Only a scrap of hair tied, we assume, around the wrist as a love token, unites the lovers. The attraction of the line lies partly in the contrast between the description of the hair as 'bright', an adjective that normally indicates abundant life, and the grave in which it is found. The alliteration of the 'b' sound also helps it to shine. Following the easy modulation of Donne's thoughts, we've been imagining the muddle of bones in earth and the muddle of bodies making love. The verse ends on a plea that the couple, likely to be separated, want one last meeting, one last 'little stay' before judgment day, when the dead will be raised.

The second verse touches on a point of religious controversy and its whole diction is a critique of Catholicism. When he refers to a 'land/where mis-devotion doth command' he is referring to countries not touched by the Reformation. In such countries the bones of saints and martyrs were venerated and were believed to work miracles of healing. In Protestant England this no longer applied. However, in a Catholic country the gravedigger, instead of leaving them alone to wait for the Last Day, would take the bones to the Bishop and have them officially declared to be the relics of saints, and so able to work miracles. By making assumption that this could only happen in countries less enlightened than his own he deftly skirts the edge of blasphemy, getting away with it by a light touch and a ready wit. Under these circumstances the lady can be Mary Magdalen (a play on Mrs Magdalen Herbert's name), the one who loved Jesus and was closest to him; Jesus having banished seven demons from the repentant woman. All women would be happy to identify themselves with Mary Magdalen and, just as the whole point of venerating the relics of saints is to have them work miracles on one's behalf, the speaker claims that this poem, which he equates with a religious document stating the case for sainthood, becomes a paper relic with its miraculous demonstration of love. Furthermore he will now show what miracles the two 'harmless lovers' have performed through their love.

In the third verse it lists their miracles, in that they loved well and faithfully; their love did not depend on sex for fulfilment and they never had sexual intercourse. In Heaven there is no marrying or giving in marriage and angels recognise no difference between the sexes. They might kiss when they meet and again when they parted but nothing took place in between. 'Our hands ne'er touched the seals Which nature, injured by late law, sets free'. By this the speaker means that human sexuality is kept suppressed under a seal, as it were, until mutual passion or 'nature' breaks down the inhibitions and brings lovers together in physical love. The moral laws of society, as well as the actual laws of the land, which are only 'late' developments compared with the long history of mankind, sternly suppress the free expression of physical love. These two lovers, however, never tried to break these 'seals'. Most forcefully, in the final couplet, the woman herself becomes the miracle and the word resonates in a more personal way. The whole tenor of the poem means that we must read the final couplet as a lover's genuine tribute, spoken in a 'words-fail-me' moment of adoration. By the end words cannot express how marvelous she is.

The Relic shows that poetry had come a long way, psychologically, from the lovers' tributes of the Elizabethan sonneteers who saw the beloved as a distant muse, flower or 'star'. Donne, though young, writes with a mature passion, and the beloved is not a distant, untouchable woman who inflames the poet almost to the point of death: she is right there in the poem, part of the grammar, holding hands with the speaker as his equal and friend in almost every pronoun ('we', 'our').

The hyperboles are carefully controlled to gain specific effects and are not the spontaneous outbursts of a young man striving to express the sense of wonder and passion surging within himself. The poem flatters the lady but makes it abundantly clear that her formal virtue was not in question. There is a logical progression of ideas and the usual dense thought, and the celebration of their enforced continence as a miracle is cleverly done. Nothing illustrates the strength, the brilliance and the economy of Donne's language more than an attempt to express his thought in ordinary, uninspired prose.

Some critics see the poem as a flippant work of Donne's early years, when he was known as 'a great visitor of ladies and a great frequenter of Playes' and the poem probably pre-dates Donne's marriage to Anne More in 1601 (when More was only 17 years old and the poet 29). The narrative certainly suggests that the lovers in the poem were very young, that they did not properly know what love was, and that their relationship was chaste: they kissed at meeting and parting, but not between meals. Is he here making fun of the superstitions attached to the purely platonic ideas of love and satirising society's blind prohibition against any physical display of love?

Whether or not Donne is writing autobiographically, believable figures move in the poem and believable emotions infuse it and, through the use of synecdoche, the woman is wonderfully present in that 'bracelet of bright hair'. Yet while we have no further details about her appearance the relationship of the young couple seems woven into the cadence of its lines so we almost experience the meeting and parting, flirting and withdrawing. Furthermore, Donne adds humour and tenderness and a striking psychological awareness to his poet's delicacy of measure and naturalness of language. If his woman is a miracle she is also a warm-blooded human companion. And we, across the centuries, experience the 'little stay' of his own human warmth. The poem certainly demonstrates his flair for boldness and daring in iconoclastic reasoning and it is a marvel that he gets away with it and eventually becomes Dean of St Paul's Cathedral.

The Sun Rising

Busy old fool, unruly Sun,
    Why dost thou thus,
Through windows, and through curtains, call on us?
Must to thy motions lovers' seasons run?
    Saucy pedantic wretch, go chide
    Late school-boys and sour prentices,
  Go tell court-huntsmen that the king will ride,
  Call country ants to harvest offices;
Love, all alike, no season knows nor clime,
Nor hours, days, months, which are the rags of time.

    Thy beams so reverend, and strong
    Why shouldst thou think?
I could eclipse and cloud them with a wink,
But that I would not lose her sight so long.
    If her eyes have not blinded thine,
    Look, and to-morrow late tell me,
  Whether both th' Indias of spice and mine
  Be where thou left'st them, or lie here with me.
Ask for those kings whom thou saw'st yesterday,
And thou shalt hear, 'All here in one bed lay.'

> She's all states, and all princes I;
> Nothing else is;
> Princes do but play us; compared to this,
> All honour's mimic, all wealth alchemy.
> Thou, Sun, art half as happy as we,
> In that the world's contracted thus;
> Thine age asks ease, and since thy duties be
> To warm the world, that's done in warming us.
> Shine here to us, and thou art everywhere;
> This bed thy center is, these walls thy sphere.

Glossary

Pendantic: fussy, sticking to the rules.
Alchemy: the discredited pseudo-science of turning base metals into gold.

Commentary

In *The Sun Rising* the speaker bluntly responds to the breaking dawn by personifying and insulting the sun with three adjectives 'Busy, old... unruly'. The first sentence is an interrogative and asks why it calls upon the couple. Donne puts the sun in its place - its job is with the working people, not with the lovers who are above the 'sour prentices' and 'country ants'. The metaphoric 'rags of time', which the sun imposes, have no meaning for couples in love.

However, there is a change of attitude in the second verse. Whereas in the first verse Donne's speaker conveys his annoyance, he now attacks the popular notion of the strong, powerful sun by pointing out that he can cut the sun out of his life merely by closing his eyes ('with a wink').

Yet even with this arrogance, he is forced to admit that without the sun, he would not be able to see his lover. And here his attitude begins to change again - through the rest of the verse it becomes less antagonistic and more complimentary to his lover and their situation together.

The line 'and tomorrow late' hints that the sun gets up too early and the mention of the 'Indias of spice and mine' is the beginning of a conceit that lasts the rest of the poem. Donne and his lover, and the room they are in, expand to become the whole world - at least, they have by the last verse.

In the third verse the conceit continues. The first two lines imply that the lovers are every country, and nothing else exists. Princes are counterfeit rulers or lovers and everything else is false, apart from the speaker and his lover. 'Thine age asks ease' returns to the idea of the 'old' sun with the speaker communicating that it must be tired from continually journeying around the world. To warm and illuminate the only true, real world, the sun need only shine in the room containing Donne and his lover.

Direct address is established in the first verse, common in Donne's poetry, and a conceit is employed, in that the lovers' bedroom becomes the world. There is also the use of sun-related imagery, such as 'eclipse and cloud' in the second verse. 'These walls, thy sphere' in verse three is also significant in that spheres were considered the perfect shape and elevates the room to a celestial level. It is also worth noting the movement in the poem. In verse one, love and the sun are separate. By verse three, Donne has joined the two - love and the sun are one and the same. With the last word Donne, his love, and the sun are gloriously united.

The Sun Rising is one of Donne's most popular poems, though the description of lovers responding to the dawn was not an uncommon subject for Elizabethan and Jacobean poets. Such poems are referred to as aubades and frequently included parting lovers. Some critics view the poem as having been written in or after 1603, with the line 'Go tell court-huntsmen that the king will ride' referencing King James, who was known to be an enthusiastic hunter.

The Triple Fool

I am two fools, I know,
    For loving, and for saying so
        In whining poetry;
But where's that wiseman, that would not be I,
    If she would not deny?
Then as th' earth's inward narrow crooked lanes
   Do purge sea water's fretful salt away,
I thought, if I could draw my pains
   Through rhyme's vexation, I should them allay.
Grief brought to numbers cannot be so fierce,
For he tames it, that fetters it in verse.

    But when I have done so,
      Some man, his art and voice to show,
        Doth set and sing my pain;
And, by delighting many, frees again
        Grief, which verse did restrain.
To love and grief tribute of verse belongs,
   But not of such as pleases when 'tis read.
Both are increased by such songs,
   For both their triumphs so are published,
And I, which was two fools, do so grow three;
Who are a little wise, the best fools be.

Glossary

Allay: to put to rest. This shows that he was trying to put his vexations to rest.

Commentary

The Triple Fool expresses the narrator's feeling that he is a fool for falling in love, for writing about that love in poetry and for making that poetry available to others to co-opt and refresh the pain that he feels. In other words, the narrator of the poem is a fool for three reasons: for loving, for expressing his love through writing, and for thinking that writing would somehow alleviate the pain and grief that he felt for being rejected.

The first stanza is the poet's way of informing the reader of what has happened and expresses how he feels. The second stanza takes the situation that the narrator is in and makes it worse by telling the reader of how his poem was published, causing his grief to be told to whoever read the poem. The second stanza develops the idea that how 'some man, his art and voice to show, doth set and sing my pain.' He explains how love and grief belong in verse, as a form of expression and coping with the emotions, but it isn't pleasing when they are sung or read aloud to others.

Personification is used in the poem with the grief the man feels personified to give it greater significance. 'Verse did restrain' his grief, as if it were an animal or another force in need of taming, hence the use of 'fetters'. Those who read the speaker's poems set free this grief to torment him again. Metaphor is used to compare the purging effects of the sea to the effects the narrator hopes his poetry will have on his pain. He wants his poetry to behave 'as th' earth's inward narrow crooked lanes,' which 'purge sea water's fretful salt away.' The 'lanes', most critics seem to agree, can be interpreted as springs or rivers. The paradoxical statements reinforce irrational love, such as 'who are a little wise, the best fools be' and the narrator continuously calls attention to the process of writing. He calls himself a fool for writing about love 'in whining poetry,' while at the same time writing about love in poetry. He then says that he 'thought, if I could draw my pains / Through rhyme's vexation, I should them allay.' In writing about this attempt, he is making the same attempt. By calling attention to the process of writing poetry, Donne gives the narrator's plight immediacy.

The poem incorporates an unusual form and rhyme scheme. It is divided into two stanzas of 11 lines each. The rhyme scheme for each stanza is aabbbcdcdee, which incorporates some half rhymes. This rhyme scheme arguably meanders to reflect the musings of the narrator over his plight.

There is a rhetorical question, 'But where's that wise man, that would not be I if she did not deny?' and asyndetic listing with 'inward, narrow, crooked lanes'. It has a self-pitying tone, full of self-criticism, though one could argue also that this is an acute but laudatory expression of self-awareness.

Twicknam Gardens

BLASTED with sighs, and surrounded with tears,
    Hither I come to seek the spring,
And at mine eyes, and at mine ears,
    Receive such balms as else cure every thing.
    But O ! self-traitor, I do bring
The spider Love, which transubstantiates all,
And can convert manna to gall ;
And that this place may thoroughly be thought
True paradise, I have the serpent brought.

'Twere wholesomer for me that winter did
    Benight the glory of this place,
And that a grave frost did forbid
    These trees to laugh and mock me to my face ;
    But that I may not this disgrace
Endure, nor yet leave loving, Love, let me
Some senseless piece of this place be ;
Make me a mandrake, so I may grow here,
Or a stone fountain weeping out my year.

Hither with crystal phials, lovers, come,
    And take my tears, which are love's wine,
And try your mistress' tears at home,
    For all are false, that taste not just like mine.
    Alas ! hearts do not in eyes shine,
Nor can you more judge women's thoughts by tears,
Than by her shadow what she wears.
O perverse sex, where none is true but she,
Who's therefore true, because her truth kills me.

Commentary

This poem was addressed to Lucy Russell, Countess of Bedford (1580-1627), who was admired as much for her learning as she was her beauty. Married at thirteen to the twenty-two-year-old earl, she was the godmother of Donne's second daughter (named Lucy in her honour). Donne, like other writers, seems to have been deeply involved with the Countess and many of his poems are thought to relate to this glamorous and accomplished woman. While known as the 'universal patroness of poets' her behavior was sometimes contradictory or provocative; her patronage could be abruptly withdrawn and, while a dedicated Calvinist, she allegedly performed bare-breasted in court masques. Apart from literary matters, the Countess was a significant figure in the development of English country-house and garden design and Twickenham Park belonged to her until 1618. She entertained a friendly affection for Donne, though whether it amounted to love on either side is impossible to say.

In *Twicknam Garden* the speaker is a forlorn and dejected lover. Even nature fails to soothe his tormented soul and the poem is a song of sorrow and despair. It expresses the anguish of a lover's heart who has fallen a prey to sadness and who cannot drown it even in nature. It is a passionate outburst of grief expressing unfulfilled love and is similar to Keats's La Belle Dame Sans Merci and Shelley's lyric, A Widow Bird Sat Mourning.

The speaker goes to Twicknam Garden in order that the beautiful sights and sounds around him might ease his anguish. But no, he finds that his bleak and desolate mood does not yield to the soothing influence of the setting. Instead, the trees mock him as he has brought the serpent into Eden.

In the first stanza a complex conceit is woven from a number of quite different religious sources. The Roman Catholic belief in transubstantiation (the transformation of bread and wine into the body and blood of Christ) is referenced with his heartache spoiling the landscape. 'Manna' is sometimes referred to as 'the bread from heaven', a reference to the Israelites being supplied with a mysterious food whilst they were travelling through the wilderness (Exodus). Here the 'spider love' is the transforming substance, but, spiders, being poisonous, make it a sort of anti-transformation: from good to bad, from bread to 'gall', a bitter substance which, mixed with vinegar, is offered to Jesus to drink while he was dying on the cross (Matthew). The final strand of the conceit is the reference to 'True Paradise', or Eden (Genesis), linking back to the serpent, a creature that turns the perfect place into a place of expulsion, grief and absence. Andrew Marvell's poem *The Garden* uses similar imagery.

The conceits in the second stanza are more straightforward: the natural image of winter being obviously in keeping with his own mood of desolation. Mandrakes had a symbolic meaning for the time: they were little plants with a forked root which were reputed to groan as they were pulled up. Some manuscripts have 'groane', some have 'grow' here. Since the groaning of mandrakes was an Elizabethan commonplace, this would appear the better reading.

In the third stanza the speaker's intellectual contempt for women is expressed in an intricate series of images. He is the stone fountain and his tears are the true tears of love. Lovers should come and take away in crystal phials these tears and compare them with those shed by their mistresses at home. If those do not taste as Donne's do, then they are not true tears of love. But there is a subtle reverse in the conceit: whereas before he was the false presence, now his tears are the sign of the true, and the tradition of hearts being reflected in eyes is decisively rejected in Donne's cynical ending. A comparison is then made with shadows, which in fact tell us little about the actual clothes a woman may be wearing. Thus he implores lovers not to be misled by the tears their mistresses shed, for you can no more judge woman's thoughts by their tears than you can judge their dresses by their shadow.

Donne ends his poem with a paradox. The woman he loves is true and chaste; she is quite honest, that is why Donne cannot enjoy her love. And it is the perversity of the female sex that the only woman who is honest and true should be the one whose honesty and truth kill the speaker, otherwise, perhaps she would not be so chaste and true.

One of the most distinguishing features of the poem is the atmosphere of sombre desolation that pervades it. The poem is steeped in grim and overwhelming despair. Blasted with sighs, and surrounded with tears, the well defined and concrete images drive home the utter despair and incurable pain of a love-lorn heart. For example the cold hardness of a 'stone fountain weeping out my tears' and 'crystal phials' leave on the mind an unforgettable impression of poignant sorrow. The frigid expression of tears gives a unifying effect to the poem. Indeed, the poet refers to tears in all the three stanzas. Tears, in fact, control the diversity of imagery that we find in the poem.

To conclude, it is worth noting that the speaker expresses his mental state in a series of attractive conceits. He is a self-traitor, as he cherishes in his bosom the spider love, which transforms everything, even the heavenly manna can be turned into poison by it. If the garden is paradise, then his passion is the serpent. He wishes to be a mandrake and grow there in the garden (for the mandrake is a plant that feels pain) or a stone fountain, for he is always weeping. In the last stanza his 'tears' are called 'Love's wine' and such conceits lend a peculiar charm to the poem.

A Valediction: Forbidding Mourning

As virtuous men pass mildly away,
   And whisper to their souls to go,
Whilst some of their sad friends do say,
   'The breath goes now,' and some say, 'No,'

So let us melt, and make no noise,
   No tear-floods, nor sigh-tempests move;
'Twere profanation of our joys
   To tell the laity our love.

Moving of the earth brings harms and fears,
   Men reckon what it did and meant;
But trepidation of the spheres,
   Though greater far, is innocent.

Dull sublunary lovers' love
   (Whose soul is sense) cannot admit
Absence, because it doth remove
   Those things which elemented it.

But we, by a love so much refined
   That our selves know not what it is,
Inter-assured of the mind,
   Care less, eyes, lips, and hands to miss.

Our two souls therefore, which are one,
   Though I must go, endure not yet
A breach, but an expansion.
   Like gold to airy thinness beat.

If they be two, they are two so
   As stiff twin compasses are two:
Thy soul, the fixed foot, makes no show
   To move, but doth, if the other do;

And though it in the center sit,
   Yet when the other far doth roam,
It leans, and hearkens after it,
   And grows erect, as that comes home.

Such wilt thou be to me, who must,
   Like the other foot, obliquely run;
Thy firmness makes my circle just,
   And makes me end where I begun.

Glossary

Valediction: a statement or address made at or as a farewell.
Profanation: sacrilegious, blasphemous act or statement.
Laity: common people. It also has religious connotations.
Trepidation: cautious, silent movement.
Sublunary: beneath the moon, of the earth, terrestrial.
Elemented: instigated, started, constructed. Also ties in with the other 'element' imagery in the poem.

Commentary

In *Valediction* we find Donne's famous compass conceit and a display of his vast knowledge, from alchemy to astronomy. There is the belief, first recorded in 1675, that it was written by Donne for his wife before he left her to travel to France, Belgium and Germany in 1611.

In the first verse the speaker urges his lover to allow them to part as though imitating the death of a virtuous man. As a virtuous man dies, he knows that he has reconciled himself to God and will therefore be accepted into heaven. He dies calmly and when the two virtuous lovers part there is to be no pain, because they know that each will be true to the other, even when they are apart. The people surrounding the dying man are quiet so as not to disturb him, just as too much outward show of emotion on the part of one lover would disturb the other or betray their love to the laity. It is therefore from a desire to part with dignity and decorum that the speaker begins.

In verse two the speaker contrasts earthquakes with the continual trepidation of the spheres. There was the Renaissance idea that there was a tremor or 'trepidation' running through the universe, or it could be interpreted as a simply a movement of the celestial spheres. The lovers are, one way or another, likened to the planets, which elevates them above the terrestrial.

The speaker is then critical of other lovers who 'cannot admit absence'. 'Dull sublunary lovers' are tied to the physical. Donne's argument is that most relationships are built on purely sensual things - if they are not together at all times, the relationship breaks down. He therefore uses the fourth verse as a point of contrast to describe a more limited type of love: a sensual love that binds lovers to the material world and thus to loss and grief.

Subsequently, the speaker asserts that the love between him and his wife is different - it is not a purely sensual relationship, but something deeper, a 'love of the mind' rather than a 'love of the body'. This love, he says, can endure even though sometimes the lovers cannot be close to each other.

Their 'love, so much refin'd' here implies pure love, and ties in with the 'pure element' (gold) imagery that Donne uses throughout the poem. Also the pure 'substance', water, is obliquely referenced: the imagery evoked by 'let us melt'. The lines 'Endure not yet / A breach', with the use of enjambment to stress the breach, imply that the only way the lovers can be parted is by death, that while they are earthbound they have but one soul.

In the seventh verse Donne contemplates the idea of two souls, rather than one and introduces his most famous conceit. The two lovers are likened to the two points of a compass. They are united and have no need of anyone else. It must also be remembered that the compass and the circle together formed the Renaissance symbol for eternal perfection. The line 'And grows erect, as it comes home' ties in with the image of the compass closing and the two points coming together, and also implies the emotional buildup of expectation and joy when the two lovers are together again. Since he is quick to denounce the obsession of the laity with the physical, there is arguably no implied sexual connotation, though we can imagine Donne relishing the ambiguity. The earlier syndetic listing of 'eyes, lips and hands' certainly foregrounds an awareness of what others will miss.

With the final two lines, 'Thy firmness makes my circle just, / And makes me end, where I began' the poet signals the completion of a circle as drawn by the compass;

only through his wife's stability in the centre is the task achieved. It also, of course, stresses his return home.

The four-line verses, or quatrains, help to give the poem a gentle, languid feel. The abab rhyme scheme is consistent and predictable all the way through. The mood of this poem is in direct contrast to that of *The Apparition*, which is raw in comparison. Here there is uncontrolled emotion, but it is confined to the 'laity', the earthly lovers who cannot stand parting.

A Valediction of Weeping

Let me pour forth
My tears before thy face, whilst I stay here,
For thy face coins them, and thy stamp they bear,
And by this mintage they are something worth,
        For thus they be
        Pregnant of thee;
Fruits of much grief they are, emblems of more,
When a tear falls, that thou falls which it bore,
So thou and I are nothing then, when on a diverse shore.

On a round ball
A workman that hath copies by, can lay
An Europe, Afric, and an Asia,
And quickly make that, which was nothing, all;
        So doth each tear
        Which thee doth wear,
A globe, yea world, by that impression grow,
Till thy tears mix'd with mine do overflow
This world; by waters sent from thee, my heaven dissolved so.

O more than moon,
Draw not up seas to drown me in thy sphere,
Weep me not dead, in thine arms, but forbear
To teach the sea what it may do too soon;
        Let not the wind

Example find,
To do me more harm than it purposeth;
Since thou and I sigh one another's breath,
Whoe'er sighs most is cruellest, and hastes the other's death.

Commentary

A valediction is an act of saying goodbye to someone. The metaphysical poem has three stanzas, each of nine lines. The lines vary in length and but do follow a specific syllabic pattern. Lines one, five and six have four syllables, lines two, three, four, seven and eight have ten and the last line in each stanza has fourteen, as if combining the previous lengths. The rhyme scheme is also complex, like the language, but has an abbaccddd pattern. Donne's fondness for rhetorical figures, paradoxes, switches in tone and ingenious conceits can make them feel artificial but in this poem he uses memorable images to convey a close relationship.

    The first person speaker addresses his lover, whom he refers to as 'thee' (the archaic form of you) and describes the grief and conflicting emotions they're about to endure. The poem begins with the narrator asking that he be allowed to cry before he parts from his lover. He wants her to see his grief and understand how his tears are created by her image. The tears also represent the spiritual connection the two share, but the actual tears are not helping their situation. His thought process on what grief is and how it should be expressed evolves and there's the warning that they should keep their emotions under control, otherwise, something terrible could happen to their relationship. Tears will bring about heaven and then its dissolution and the narrator tells his listener not to drown him in her grief. By weeping and sighing she will endanger him; in short, the grief of one is liable to condemn the other to death. The woman, as is the case with most of Donne's poetry, is not given a voice and therefore her response is not known.

    The poem makes use of several literary devices, some of which are crucial to its categorization as metaphysical, but the dominant extended metaphor - or conceit - is that of tears, and their meaning in terms of grief, identity and perception. The tears are described in powerful, worldly terms and are linked to globes, spheres and seas. They are also imbued with a number of powers and features and the narrator is completely consumed by the use of tears and their effect on the world. There is the argument that the listener's image and essence, within the falling tears, has the ability to dissolve them into nothingness.

With the title of the poem, it is clear a parting is soon to occur and the couple clearly have limited time left together. The tears which fall from the narrator have their source in the listener's face. Her visage, heart, and spiritual being 'coins them' or creates them. Rolling down his cheeks, they bear the 'stamp' of the addressee. The tears are also 'pregnant' with the listener and this metaphor of production continues and expands and the tears soon become more like fruit than coins. As the tears fall away from the narrator, making the tears worthless as they are no longer a part of him, the addressee falls too. The worthless nature of fallen tears leads them to diverse shores, a separation which leads to nothing.

In the second stanza the speaker begins by referring to the globe as 'a round ball', smaller in scale than the earth and therefore easier for a workman to 'lay / An Europe, Afric, and an Asia' on its surface. It is only when the landmasses are present on the surface, that the sphere has meaning. This is how the speaker sees his and the addressee's tears, yet when they combine with the speaker's and 'overflow' they become too much for either of them to bear, leading to disastrous consequences. The reference to a globe continues in the final stanza with the moon. The addressee is 'more than the moon' and has similar powers. The request not to 'Draw…up seas to drown [him]' also links her to the moon and the tides and argues that they should refrain from weeping, as her tears and sighs will instruct the sea and wind.

The piece to have been written after Donne's secret marriage in 1601, during a period of separation. His marriage often surfaces obliquely within his poetry, especially due to the impact it had on his career and his short imprisonment in Fleet Prison.

Elegy V. His Picture

Here take my picture; though I bid farewell
Thine, in my heart, where my soul dwells, shall dwell.
'Tis like me now, but I dead, 'twill be more
When we are shadows both, than 'twas before.
When weather-beaten I come back, my hand
Perhaps with rude oars torn, or sun beams tann'd,
My face and breast of haircloth, and my head
With care's rash sudden storms being o'erspread,
My body a sack of bones, broken within,
And powder's blue stains scatter'd on my skin;
If rival fools tax thee to have loved a man
So foul and coarse as, oh, I may seem then,
This shall say what I was, and thou shalt say,
'Do his hurts reach me? Doth my worth decay?
Or do they reach his judging mind, that he
Should now love less, what he did love to see?
That which in him was fair and delicate,
Was but the milk which in love's childish state
Did nurse it; who now is grown strong enough
To feed on that, which to disused tastes seems tough.'

Commentary

Elegie 5. His Picture is a valedictory poem in which the speaker gives his loved one his portrait as a parting gift. The goodbye is dignified and tender. Furthermore, the parting presupposes that the speaker is going to war and that he may be gone for several years. When he returns they may both be 'shadows,' and he will perhaps be emaciated, prematurely grey and powder-stained. This imaginative, somewhat melodramatic preview of himself as a returned soldier, suggests a contrast between the young man of the picture and what he will grow into. It further permits the analogy of childish love to 'grown' love.

His picture is, metaphorically, his youthful appearance, in much the same manner as the 'image' in *Elegy X. The Dream*. The picture is used to suggest that lovers' images or actual pictures are present in each other's hearts during absence: 'Here take my picture; though I bid farewell. / Thine, in my heart, where my soul dwells, shall dwell.

As the speaker presents the actual picture to his loved one, he promises her that should he die, the image will become more like him than he is at present. For when they are both shadows of their present state, his picture will be all the reality left of him. Moreover, the picture will be tangible evidence of the handsome man he is, rather than the scratched, tanned and unshaven man he may be when he returns from the war. For some critics there is the use of 'bold synecdoche' in the line 'my head with cares rash sudden storms, being o'espread' with the speaker's premature greyness implied as though fallen snow had whitened the hair.

The 'picture' metaphor gives an easily perceived time dimension to the poem. In the present the picture is a representation of the speaker as he is. In the future, with its hard facts of separation and war, the picture will be the interchanged image of lasting love between them. And when at his return people argue that she is a fool to love a wornout, weather-beaten man, she will say:

Doe his hurt reach me? doth my worth decay?
Or do they reach his judging mind, that he
Should now love less, what he did love to see?

In other words, now that he has matured will he see her less physically beautiful, 'what he did love to see?'

That which in him was fair and delicate.
Was but the milk, which in love's childish state
Did nurse it: who now is grown strong enough
To feed on that which to disused tastes seems tough.

In these lines love is personified as requiring milk (physical beauty), but who, upon maturity, can digest the unaccustomed food of a tough diet. The metaphor, then, has its foundations in the Platonic belief that beauty, comprehended through the senses, i.e. the initial and proper beginning of love. In their love's beginning, physical beauty was milk, the proper food. However, their love will have become more spiritualized, more mature, and no longer will be dependent upon physical beauty or the senses.

The picture, then, is the depth metaphor of the poem, and the resulting paradox rises from it. In the first place, the lovers are not really separated even though they are apart. There will be a bond between them always. And the speaker's actual appearance, when returned from war, as contrasted to his fairness when he was young, will be symbolic of the couple's mature love. War, trouble, time, and separation will have a beneficent value here, for paradoxically, the suffering they bring will refine the love of the speaker and his beloved.

Song: Go and Catch a Falling Star

Go and catch a falling star,
Get with child a mandrake root,
Tell me where all past years are,
Or who cleft the devil's foot,
Teach me to hear mermaids singing,
Or to keep off envy's stinging,
    And find
    What wind
Serves to advance an honest mind.

If thou be'st born to strange sights,
Things invisible to see,
Ride ten thousand days and nights,
Till age snow white hairs on thee,
Thou, when thou return'st, wilt tell me,

All strange wonders that befell thee,
    And swear,
    No where
Lives a woman true, and fair.

If thou find'st one, let me know,
Such a pilgrimage were sweet;
Yet do not, I would not go,
Though at next door we might meet;
Though she were true, when you met her,
And last, till you write your letter,
    Yet she
    Will be
False, ere I come, to two, or three.

Commentary

First published in 1633, *Go and Catch a Falling Star* is a merciless take on a traditional theme: women's infidelity. It's an unusual Donne poem in that nothing redeems the evident misogyny. There are no extended metaphors, the language is robust, the meter is relatively steady and the imperatives are tripping over each other. Its message is simple, the first-person narrator tells a listener that he can search the whole wide world, but finding an attractive woman who'll remain faithful to him is an impossible task. The poem's use of hyperbole make its tone feel somewhat light-hearted and frivolous, but the narrator seems to harbour a bitterness towards women.

    In summary, he advises the listener to catch a 'falling star', impregnate a mandrake root (a tuber which can resemble a human and thought to have magical qualities), find where the past years go, or discover who cleft (split) the devil's hoof in two. Similarly, the reader/listener is commanded to hear mermaids singing (possibly a reference to the sirens of Greek mythology), find a cure for the 'sting' of envy, and what wind exists that can help 'an honest mind' to get on in life.

    In the second stanza, the narrator tells the addressee that if he is born to see strange sights and invisible things then he must ride for ten thousand days (27 years) till he's old and his hair is white. He'll then be prepared to swear that faithful women who are 'fair' (attractive) do not exist. Yet if the listener does find such a woman, he should tell the narrator, who would journey to meet her. But then the narrator changes his mind. He wouldn't go, even if she lived next door, because even if she stayed faithful long enough for the listener to write the letter describing her to the narrator, she'd inevitably have cheated on two or three lovers by the time the narrator arrived.

In conclusion, the vivid images in the first verse all have transgressive and/or sexual connotations. They create a clear picture of a world full of impossible tasks and brimming over with sexual deviance. It does all this in the form of an apostrophe. The narrator is commanding his listener to go out and perform these tasks, using an insistent trochaic meter (meaning the lines follow a stressed-unstressed pattern). However, the final trochees are cut short, thus beginning and ending the line on a stressed beat. This unrelenting beat helps to set the tone, making the poem both forceful and light, imaginative and resigned, beautiful and ugly.

Song: Sweetest Love, I Do Not Go

Sweetest love, I do not go,
    For weariness of thee,
Nor in hope the world can show
    A fitter love for me;
        But since that I
Must die at last, 'tis best
To use myself in jest
        Thus by feign'd deaths to die.

Yesternight the sun went hence,
    And yet is here today;
He hath no desire nor sense,
    Nor half so short a way:
        Then fear not me,

But believe that I shall make
Speedier journeys, since I take
    More wings and spurs than he.

O how feeble is man's power,
    That if good fortune fall,
Cannot add another hour,
    Nor a lost hour recall!
        But come bad chance,
And we join to'it our strength,
And we teach it art and length,
    Itself o'er us to'advance.

When thou sigh'st, thou sigh'st not wind,
    But sigh'st my soul away;
When thou weep'st, unkindly kind,
    My life's blood doth decay.
        It cannot be
That thou lov'st me, as thou say'st,
If in thine my life thou waste,
    That art the best of me.

Let not thy divining heart
    Forethink me any ill;
Destiny may take thy part,
    And may thy fears fulfil;
        But think that we
Are but turn'd aside to sleep;
They who one another keep
    Alive, ne'er parted be.

Commentary

Sweetest Love I Do Not Go was first published in 1633 and it reveals the pain of separation from a loved one. The narrator's words to his lover are said to reassure her. He is not tired of her, or looking for another lover or trying to run away from her. Their separation is a pretend death and his return is as inevitable as that of the rising sun. The comparison to the sun is extended and without 'desire' or 'sense' there is equally nothing which will distract him from his mission. Moreover, while they are similar in their steadfastness, the narrator is much faster than the sun and is going to swiftly accomplish his journey because he has 'More wings and spurs.'

    The narrator concludes by asking his lover not to cry or sigh over him as this could endanger him if 'Destiny' acts in response to any 'ill' feelings she might have. Rather than harm him, the narrator asks that his lover imagine that they are in bed together with their backs turned towards one another. It ends with the message that those who keep one another alive, be it only in their thoughts, will never be parted. The narrator's tone throughout is confident and determined, but suitably loving. He does everything he can to convince her that they can endure the separation and will be reunited once more. The five verses are each of eight lines long (an octave) and follow a pattern of ababcddc. The lines vary in length, but each verse is separated into two sets of four lines, (therefore an octave consisting of two quatrains). A new but related topic is introduced in the fifth line.

A Nocturnal Upon St Lucy's Day, Being the Shortest Day

'Tis the year's midnight, and it is the day's,
Lucy's, who scarce seven hours herself unmasks;
    The sun is spent, and now his flasks
    Send forth light squibs, no constant rays;
        The world's whole sap is sunk;
The general balm th' hydroptic earth hath drunk,
Whither, as to the bed's feet, life is shrunk,
Dead and interr'd; yet all these seem to laugh,
Compar'd with me, who am their epitaph.

Study me then, you who shall lovers be
At the next world, that is, at the next spring;
    For I am every dead thing,

       In whom Love wrought new alchemy.
           For his art did express
A quintessence even from nothingness,
From dull privations, and lean emptiness;
He ruin'd me, and I am re-begot
Of absence, darkness, death: things which are not.

All others, from all things, draw all that's good,
Life, soul, form, spirit, whence they being have;
     I, by Love's limbec, am the grave
     Of all that's nothing. Oft a flood
         Have we two wept, and so
Drown'd the whole world, us two; oft did we grow
To be two chaoses, when we did show
Care to aught else; and often absences
Withdrew our souls, and made us carcasses.

But I am by her death (which word wrongs her)
Of the first nothing the elixir grown;
     Were I a man, that I were one
     I needs must know; I should prefer,
         If I were any beast,
Some ends, some means; yea plants, yea stones detest,
And love; all, all some properties invest;
If I an ordinary nothing were,
As shadow, a light and body must be here.

But I am none; nor will my sun renew.
You lovers, for whose sake the lesser sun
     At this time to the Goat is run
     To fetch new lust, and give it you,
         Enjoy your summer all;
Since she enjoys her long night's festival,
Let me prepare towards her, and let me call
This hour her vigil, and her eve, since this
Both the year's, and the day's deep midnight is.

Glossary

Hydroptic: containing excessive water or fluid
Epitaph: words that are written or said about a dead person, especially words on a gravestone
Limbec: a still/to distill

Commentary

A 'nocturnal' refers to events or happenings during the night and the poem is a reflective meditation on the night of St. Lucy's day (13th December), the shortest day before the Gregorian calendar reforms. The day is sacred to the memory of St. Lucy, martyred for her choice of spiritual love over physical love. The name Lucy, derived from the Latin word for light also gives the poem an ironic twist given that the long night intensifies the darkness in the narrator's heart.

In the poem Donne uses the imagery of the Winter Solstice as a symbol of mourning someone beloved as well as, with the light beginning to return, a spiritual celebration and rebirth. With no evidence of when Donne wrote the poem, it is not known if he was writing about Lucy Russell, Countess of Bedford (1580-1627), a daughter who died, or Anne More who died in 1617 in childbirth with their twelfth child.

However, what can be said for certain is that the wintery darkness is an apt setting for reflecting on the spiritual anguish and sorrow felt by the narrator and that the contemplation on loss is a scholarly and fluent meditation with lines flowing freely. The poem has five stanzas of nine lines each and has a familiar rhyme scheme of abbacccdd. One short line in the middle of each stanza (line five) comes as a welcome break and acts as a rhetorical device which suits the structure of the poem. With lines of unequal length there is arguably a lightness which elevates it above being a merely a rigid and melancholic diatribe.

In the poem the eponymous saint, like the sun, shows her face for seven hours When the sun sets the stars (his flasks) give forth dim flickering light. The whole world has lost its vitality. The earth has drunk the vigour of nature, its sap is at the lowest, while the earth is swollen with water and snow. All of life lies like a dead man's body, cold and shrunk; all is dead and buried. The narrator, alone and aware of nature's regenerative power, acts as an epitaph. In the second stanza the narrator tells those who would love to notice his condition and compare it with the condition in the spring when life shall return. He is like the dead, in a state of nothingness, left without his beloved. The narrator pursues this line of thought in the third stanza when he states that Love personified once worked upon him, but Love has now turned him 'into the grave / Of all that's nothing'. He then reflects upon their relationship and talks of tears enough to drown the world and how, being apart from one another, they became just corpses.

  In the fourth stanza his lament continues and the burden of thought and feeling is explored, preferring to be an animal or a thing having one quality or another. In the final stanza the narrator's condition of absolute nothingness is established. He urges other lovers to enjoy their summer of lust while he, in the present hour, will hold a vigil – a period of prayer – as if expecting her resurrection or for death to reunite them.

A Hymn to God the Father

Wilt thou forgive that sin where I begun,
  Which was my sin, though it were done before?
Wilt thou forgive that sin, through which I run,
  And do run still, though still I do deplore?
    When thou hast done, thou hast not done,
      For I have more.

Wilt thou forgive that sin which I have won
  Others to sin, and made my sin their door?
Wilt thou forgive that sin which I did shun
  A year or two, but wallow'd in, a score?
    When thou hast done, thou hast not done,

> For I have more.
>
> I have a sin of fear, that when I have spun
>   My last thread, I shall perish on the shore;
> But swear by thyself, that at my death thy Son
>   Shall shine as he shines now, and heretofore;
>   And, having done that, thou hast done;
>   I fear no more.

Commentary

A Hymn to God the Father, also titled *To Christ*, is one of Donne's Divine Poems, posthumously published in 1688. The poem, one of his most famous religious works, is similar to several of the Holy Sonnets in that it doesn't set out to praise God, but rather engages him in debate. The narrator is not aiming to sing God's praises uncritically, but questions God about sin and forgiveness. The rhyme scheme of ababab seems to reinforce this idea of question-and-answer and we might summarise the narrator's argument as one which escalates with each question. For example, the poem begins with asking for forgiveness for sins committed before he was born (Original Sin), but by the second verse the narrator is asking to be forgiven for leading others into sin. It ends with the sin of fear - specifically fear of death - but if God, that the narrator will see his son, Jesus Christ, shining and there to save him, then all is all right and he will 'fear no more.'

    In the final verse 'I have a sin of fear' is a clever inversion of what the reader might expect, which is to have a fear of sin. Donne employs his ability to argue a case superbly in the poem, not least by opening his case by blaming Adam and Eve. The narrator is weak for following their example, but in a sense he is only being human. Moreover, Donne puns on his own name throughout (remember after marrying – and ending up in Fleet prison – how he bitterly punned: 'John Donne, Anne Donne, Un-done'). The word Donne/done also fits nicely with the idea of things being predetermined (or already 'done') thanks to Original Sin. It is also worth noting that after four interrogatives, the narrator ends with an imperative, demanding that God 'swear by thyself'. Such an irreverent ending suits the poem which is refreshing in its directness, and no-nonsense approach.

The Indifferent

I can love both fair and brown,
Her whom abundance melts, and her whom want betrays,
Her who loves loneness best, and her who masks and plays,
Her whom the country formed, and whom the town,
Her who believes, and her who tries,
Her who still weeps with spongy eyes,
And her who is dry cork, and never cries;
I can love her, and her, and you, and you,
I can love any, so she be not true.

Will no other vice content you?
Will it not serve your turn to do as did your mothers?
Or have you all old vices spent, and now would find out others?
Or doth a fear that men are true torment you?
O we are not, be not you so;
Let me, and do you, twenty know.
Rob me, but bind me not, and let me go.
Must I, who came to travail thorough you,
Grow your fixed subject, because you are true?

Venus heard me sigh this song,
And by love's sweetest part, variety, she swore,
She heard not this till now; and that it should be so no more.
She went, examined, and returned ere long,
And said, Alas! some two or three
Poor heretics in love there be,
Which think to 'stablish dangerous constancy.
But I have told them, Since you will be true,
You shall be true to them who are false to you.

Commentary

In *The Indifferent* the narrator boasts that he can love all sorts of women, that he is 'indifferent' to whom he loves because physical pleasure exists - and is wonderful - for its own sake. It is a relatively simple love poem in comparison to his other, more complicated works. In the poem he presents a lover who regards constancy as a 'vice' and promiscuity as the path of virtue and good sense. Because of Donne's Christian background, this poem was obviously meant to be a comical look at values that were opposite the ones held by Christians. According to the critic Clay Hunt, The Indifferent is probably quite an early poem because of the simplicity and obviousness of its literary methods, its untroubled gaiety, and its pose of libertinism, which all suggest that Donne wrote the poem when he was a young man about town in Elizabethan London.

The Holy Sonnets

The Holy or Divine Sonnets are a series of nineteen poems which were first published in 1633, two years after Donne's death. They generally follow the pattern set down by the Italian poet Petrarch (1304–1374) with an octave (an eight-line stanza or, on occasion, two quatrains) and a sestet (a six-line stanza). However, the inclusion of a rhyming couplet at the end reflects Shakespeare's influence on the sonnet form.

Many of the poems are thought to have been written between 1609 and 1610, when Donne was converting from Roman Catholicism to the Protestant church, and the Holy Sonnets understandably address several religious themes, including divine love, divine judgment and mortality. Several composers have set the sonnets to music, including Benjamin Britten (1913–1976) Britten composed his own songs in 1945 for tenor Peter Pears, his lover and musical collaborator, having been 'encouraged...to explore the work of Donne' by W.H. Auden.

Sonnets are often, although not always, about ideals or hypothetical situations. They are made up of fourteen lines, each being ten syllables long. In a Petrarchan or Italian sonnet eight lines of two quatrains make up the first section of the sonnet (the octave). The octave will often explore a problem or an idea. The following six lines (the sestet), form a response or counter-view. A Shakespearean sonnet usually contains three quatrains, the first twelve lines), followed by a rhyming couplet. The rhyming couplet resolves any issue or debate and sometimes functions almost like a punchline. Both types of sonnet can contain a 'turn' or volta. In a Petrarchan this is likely to appear at the end of the octave, in a Shakespearean it can arise at the start of the couplet. Sonnets are written in is iambic pentameter (five iambs per line, where a iamb is one unstressed followed by one stressed syllable).Each line should therefore be made up of ten syllables.

Holy Sonnet I: Thou hast made me, and shall thy work decay?

Thou hast made me, and shall thy work decay?
Repair me now, for now mine end doth haste,
I run to death, and death meets me as fast,
And all my pleasures are like yesterday;
I dare not move my dim eyes any way,
Despair behind, and death before doth cast
Such terror, and my feebled flesh doth waste
By sin in it, which it towards hell doth weigh.
Only thou art above, and when towards thee
By thy leave I can look, I rise again;
But our old subtle foe so tempteth me,
That not one hour I can myself sustain;
Thy grace may wing me to prevent his art,
And thou like adamant draw mine iron heart.

Commentary

The sonnet opens with an interrogative, asking if God's going to allow his creation, the narrator, to fall into 'decay.' The following line is a bold imperative, demanding that God repairs him. The tone is impatient, with little time to waste. The narrator is running towards death, and it is coming 'fast' to meet him. All pleasure lies in the past and the future only holds the terror of death. His 'dim' eyes – dim because he's old – fear to look backwards or forwards. His past has infected him with sin and weighs him towards hell.

However, in the sestet the narrator's tone becomes somewhat more hopeful. When he looks towards God he feels elevated, or at least rises above his sinful state. And yet the 'subtle old foe', Satan, is still tempting him. Again, one might argue that this is an autobiographical poem. We do know that Donne suffered greatly towards the end of his life and that much of his youth was spent in the pursuit of pleasure. Yet he embraced a religious life after the death of his wife and ultimately became Dean of St Paul's Cathedral.

The sonnet concludes with the narrator inviting God to 'wing' or fly him away from sin (here the noun wing is used as a verb, an example of anthimeria). And in the final line the narrator likens God to a magnet and talks of his own 'iron heart'. He is thus drawn, and always has been, to God's grace. This metaphysical conceit certainly gives the sonnet a powerful ending. The octave therefore presents the problem of temptation, and the sestet presents the solution as being God's power and attraction.

The sonnet's rhyme scheme can be interpreted as abbaabba cdcdee, though the octave appears to contain two half rhymes (appears because an alternative pronunciation should be considered). The form is largely Petrarchan with its octave and sestet. However, Donne's choice of cdcdee, albeit a common one, deviates from what can be strictly defined as Petrarchan sonnet, the sestet here ending with a couplet.

Holy Sonnet V - I Am A Little World Made Cunningly

I am a little world made cunningly
Of elements and an angelic sprite,
But black sin hath betray'd to endless night
My world's both parts, and oh both parts must die.
You which beyond that heaven which was most high
Have found new spheres, and of new lands can write,
Pour new seas in mine eyes, that so I might
Drown my world with my weeping earnestly,
Or wash it, if it must be drown'd no more.
But oh it must be burnt; alas the fire
Of lust and envy have burnt it heretofore,
And made it fouler; let their flames retire,
And burn me O Lord, with a fiery zeal
Of thee and thy house, which doth in eating heal.

Commentary

The sonnet starts with the narrator asserting that a human is essentially a soul, or spirit who possesses a body made of 'elements'. He is pleading with God to release him from the pain of his sins, to be cleansed, so that he may unite with his creator. The narrator is prepared to suffer drowning and burning to erase his past misdeeds. The tone is miserable and guilt-ridden. For some it might be seen as autobiographical as Donne struggled to control his sexual appetite in his younger years, therefore making it easy to interpret the feelings of guilt as stemming from his youth within many of his religious sonnets.
      The rhyme scheme here is abba cddc efef gg; which could be defined as three quatrains, with a rhyming couplet at the end. However, unlike most sonnets there is no clear turn or 'volta', although the punishment turns to burning and is marked by the fronting conjunction 'But'. The metrical rhythm broadly keeps to iambic pentameter, that is five beats in the line starting with an unstressed syllable. However, line thirteen is anapaestic: two unstressed followed by one stressed syllable.

The imagery within the sonnet creates a world made up of seas and lands and spheres as well as one of punishment by fire and water. The poet conveys a mood of desperation and yet within the penultimate line there is the strong desire to be consumed by a holy 'fiery zeal'.

Holy Sonnet VI - This is My Play's Last Scene

This is my play's last scene; here heavens appoint
My pilgrimage's last mile; and my race,
Idly, yet quickly run, hath this last pace,
My span's last inch, my minute's latest point;
And gluttonous death will instantly unjoint
My body and my soul, and I shall sleep a space;
But my'ever-waking part shall see that face
Whose fear already shakes my every joint.
Then, as my soul to heaven, her first seat, takes flight,
And earth-born body in the earth shall dwell,
So fall my sins, that all may have their right,
To where they are bred, and would press me, to hell.
Impute me righteous, thus purg'd of evil,
For thus I leave the world, the flesh, the devil.

Glossary

Impute: attribute something to someone (normally with negative connotations).

Commentary

The sonnet is thought to have been written between 1607-9 and is therefore not quite the deathbed poem it appears to be on first reading. However, it does deal with death, life and salvation in a way that expresses Donne's own religious views. Comparing life to a play, a race and a pilgrimage, the narrator accepts the inevitability of death, but believes that his sins will remain on earth while his soul flies up to heaven. Metaphors abound in the octave, with 'playes last scene', 'pilgrimages last mile' and 'my race quickly runne', underlining his time on Earth is coming to an end and that a greedy death is waiting impatiently to consume his flesh. It is also worth saying that he frames his life as 'my pilgrimage' to suggest a life lived with God in mind. The common euphemism for death, 'sleep', is then employed, as is 'space' for the grave, before the fronting conjunction in the fifth line.

As explained later on, his 'earth-born body' will remain there forever with the soul shedding its sins and leaving them behind where they were 'bred'. But before the narrator takes his 'first seat', which suggests that our souls originated from heaven, he must face his God. The following sestet is therefore employed to demonstrate the divinity of his soul and the importance of Christ's sacrifice, by which mankind's sins were purged. In the final line the soul is shown by death to be freed from the triple threat of earthly sin which consists of 'the world, the flesh, the devil' and returns to its divine roots. 'Impute' or label me 'righteous', but the narrator is confident that his soul, as will others, will be cleansed to an envious degree. It could be argued, however, that the narrator's certainty of his own ascension is due to his immovable faith in his own morality and the sonnet is therefore a criticism of earthly society as well as a warning to those who are not leading a pilgrim's life.

While the poem is clearly another Donne sonnet with the familiar abba abba cddc ee, rhyme scheme, the volta or 'turn' is a matter of debate. The octave ends with a full stop, as one expects after line eight, and the flight to heaven begins, yet there is a different tone in the last four lines, which have something of a prayer-like quality. Furthermore, line nine, is a twelve rather than a ten syllable line. This disrupts the flow of the sonnet, as does the use of enjambment in the opening quatrain, which arguably slows it down to a contemplative state that reflects a sharp awareness of the final act and the subsequent judgement.

Holy Sonnet VII: At the Round Earth's Imagined Corners, Blow

At the round earth's imagin'd corners, blow
Your trumpets, angels, and arise, arise
From death, you numberless infinities
Of souls, and to your scatter'd bodies go;
All whom the flood did, and fire shall o'erthrow,
All whom war, dearth, age, agues, tyrannies,
Despair, law, chance hath slain, and you whose eyes
Shall behold God and never taste death's woe.
But let them sleep, Lord, and me mourn a space,
For if above all these my sins abound,
'Tis late to ask abundance of thy grace
When we are there; here on this lowly ground
Teach me how to repent; for that' as good
As if thou hadst seal'd my pardon with thy blood.

Commentary

Donne's title and first line is contradictory, with 'the round earth's imagined corners.' The world was known to be round by the early 17th century, but angels appear in the corners because everyone needs to hear the trumpets. Moreover, Renaissance maps often had angels blowing trumpets from the north, south, east, and west. The opening sentence creates an image in the reader's mind but the it also functions as an imperative with the narrator commanding angels and the dead to 'arise'. It's Judgment Day and the trumpets will awaken the souls of the souls of the dead to be reunited with their corpses.

However, in the sestet, which opens with the familiar fronting conjunction, 'But', the narrator then reveals he feels he's been too hasty: 'But let them sleep' (sleep being a common euphemism for death). The narrator wants time to mourn over his own grave, 'space', and to fully repent his sins. He asks God to teach him how to atone for his sins, worried that he hasn't repented sufficiently on earth and that his own sins might be greater than those who are at peace. If God can teach him how to repent, it would be as if God had signed a pardon with his own blood, which, fittingly and reassuringly, God has already done having sent his son into the world to shed his blood for the sins of mankind.

The sonnet alludes to two sections of the Book of Revelation. The first sentence of Revelation 7 is 'After this I saw four angels standing at the four corners of the earth, holding back the four winds of the earth to prevent any wind from blowing on the land or on the sea.' And the second sentence of Revelation 8, which mentions seven angels standing before God with their trumpets. What Donne is creating is the Last Judgement. In Christian theology, the soul and body are separated when you die, but are reunited on Judgment Day. The 'numberless infinities' obviously includes all those who have died in history. There's a reference to those who drowned during the flood, which only Noah and his family survived, as well as those who will be consumed in the 'fires' that end the world (though the righteous will not 'taste death's woe'). The word 'dearth' indicates people who have died of hunger, while 'agues' means sickness.

Holy Sonnet X: Death, Be Not Proud

Death, be not proud, though some have called thee
Mighty and dreadful, for thou are not so;
For those whom thou think'st thou dost overthrow
Die not, poor Death, nor yet canst thou kill me.
From rest and sleep, which but thy pictures be,
Much pleasure; then from thee much more must flow,
And soonest our best men with thee do go,
Rest of their bones, and soul's delivery.
Thou'art slave to fate, chance, kings, and desperate men,
And dost with poison, war, and sickness dwell,
And poppy'or charms can make us sleep as well
And better than thy stroke; why swell'st thou then?
One short sleep past, we wake eternally,
And death shall be no more; Death, thou shalt die.

Commentary

Death Be Not Proud, also known as *Sonnet X*, is a sonnet which, critics believe, was written between February and August 1609. However, the poem was not published during Donne's lifetime and but published posthumously in 1633. It is included as one of the nineteen sonnets that comprise Donne's Holy Sonnets or Divine Meditations. Most editions number the poem as the tenth in the sonnet sequence, which follows the order of poems in the Westmoreland Manuscript (circa 1620), the most complete arrangement of the cycle, discovered in the late nineteenth century.

Donne suffered a major illness that brought him close to death during his eighth year as an Anglican minister. The illness may have been typhoid fever, but in recent years it has been shown that he may have had a relapsing fever in combination with other illnesses. The sonnet has an abba abba cdd caa rhyme scheme. The last line alludes to 1 Corinthians 15:26: 'The last enemy that shall be destroyed is death'.

The poem was set for voice and piano by Benjamin Britten as the concluding song in his cycle *The Holy Sonnets* of John Donne. The Metaphysics within the poem, the study of the reality beyond the everyday world, is clear and there are hardly any images of the physical world which we're so used to seeing. It uses philosophical arguments, rather than descriptions of nature, and the speaker is addressing Death, the only thing positioned between the speaker and eternal bliss.

Holy Sonnet XI: Spit in My Face You Jews, and Pierce My Side

Spit in my face, you Jews, and pierce my side,
Buffet, and scoff, scourge, and crucify me,
For I have sinn'd, and sinne', and only He,
Who could do no iniquity, hath died.
But by my death can not be satisfied
My sins, which pass the Jews' impiety.

They kill'd once an inglorious man, but I
Crucify him daily, being now glorified.
O let me then His strange love still admire;
Kings pardon, but He bore our punishment;
And Jacob came clothed in vile harsh attire,
But to supplant, and with gainful intent;
God clothed Himself in vile man's flesh, that so
He might be weak enough to suffer woe.

Commentary

In *Spit in My Face, You Jews* the narrator utilizes the title, which is not uncommon within sonnets. The line is shocking, but the subject becomes clear almost immediately. The narrator likens himself to Jesus Christ and invites the Jews (who killed Jesus) to insult and kill him too. He labels himself a sinner and declares that he, unlike the Jews, daily crucifies Christ. Earlier, the difference between the narrator and Christ is also emphasised by the fact that Jesus 'could do no iniquity' or wrong. Moreover, the narrator's death will not remove his or anybody else's sins. Lines eleven and twelve refer to Jacob and his clothing himself in the skin of goats in order to gain his father's blessing. These lines introduce the idea of transformation, which is extended with God having clothed himself in human flesh in order to be amongst them and spread his message. This allowed his son to 'suffer woe' and to die for sins of mankind.

The structure of this sonnet should now be familiar, though it is worth mentioning that enjambment, which occurs when a line runs on, is clear in the penultimate and last line of the octave, placing the emphasis on the word 'Crucify' in order to shock the reader. Caesura, or pauses in the middle of lines, can be identified in lines twelve and thirteen, giving Spit in my face, you Jews a confessional tone with lines which almost stumble in delivery.

Holy Sonnet XIV: Batter My Heart, Three-Person'd God

Batter my heart, three-person'd God, for you
As yet but knock, breathe, shine, and seek to mend;
That I may rise and stand, o'erthrow me, and bend
Your force to break, blow, burn, and make me new.
I, like an usurp'd town to another due,
Labour to admit you, but oh, to no end;
Reason, your viceroy in me, me should defend,
But is captiv'd, and proves weak or untrue.
Yet dearly I love you, and would be lov'd fain,
But am betroth'd unto your enemy;
Divorce me, untie or break that knot again,
Take me to you, imprison me, for I,
Except you enthrall me, never shall be free,
Nor ever chaste, except you ravish me.

Commentary

The 14th sonnet belongs to a series Donne wrote between 1609 and 1611 during a period of religious conversion from Catholicism to Anglicanism. They are religious in nature, and deal with themes like faith, death and divine love. In this particular poem, the narrator has lost his faith altogether and prays desperately for God's return. The phrase 'three person'd God' in this devotional poem is an allusion to the Holy Trinity: the Father, the Son (Jesus), and the Holy Spirit. The word 'Batter' suggests battering rams and this word choice, thus compares the speaker's heart to a fortress that must be broken into. The opening use of an apostrophe (an address to a being that cannot respond) gives the poem the quality of a prayer and yet – paradoxically – commanding God is not a particularly pious or reverent thing to do. There's an irony here, in that the narrator wants to be faithful and to serve God.

In keeping with the sonnet form the poem has fourteen lines of rhymed iambic pentameter. Its rhyme scheme and structure is based on that used by Petrarch, with an octave and a sestet, yet it ends with a Shakespearean rhyming couplet. In the octave logical thinking is held captive but the narrator desires to be loved by God, despite being married to his enemy. God needs to enslave the narrator or he'll never be free or pure, unless God has his way with him. The root of the problem is not so much that the narrator doesn't believe in God, but rather that he cannot feel God in heart and soul, as he once did.

The narrator then compares his soul to a 'usurp'd town'. The usurper is unspecified, but could be the devil, or atheism. God must break into the town to set the narrator free. Faith, it seems, is beyond the narrator's control. God must invade that fortress to transform the narrator back into a devout Christian. Erotic desire or a desire for ecstasy on a spiritual level then surfaces with the invitation for a rough - and consensual - seduction, one that fills the speaker with such passion that it eradicates all doubt. It is only through such passion, rather than logic or reason, that the narrator can truly overcome his crisis of faith. Passion is central to faith and there is clearly the need in the sonnet to feel passionate love for God in order to believe in him.

In the middle of the sonnet it is clear that the narrator wants to be with God, but is 'betroth'd' or married, to God's 'enemy'. This enemy can be interpreted as the devil or atheism. At the end of the octave the narrator says 'Reason, your viceroy in me, me should defend, / But is captiv'd, and proves weak or untrue'. Here, 'Reason' should be providing arguments for faith in God, but it is swayed by other arguments. In the final six lines the narrator issues a series of demands, including 'Divorce me', 'break that knot again' and 'imprison me'. Having 'Ravish' as the penultimate word in a religious poem is startling with its sexual undertones. It conveys the desire for a rough, spiritual seduction and yet it acts as a suitable climax for an increasingly passionate plea for God to intervene forcefully.

Donne Timeline

- 1572 John Donne is born
- 1590 Spenser's Faerie Queene (I-III) is published
- 1591 Increasing persecution of Catholics. Kyd writes *The Spanish Tragedy*, thought to have a strong influence on Shakespeare's *Hamlet*.
- 1592 Donne goes to Lincoln's Inn to study law.
- 1593 Theatres closed because of plague.
- 1596 Essex attacks Cadiz. Second Blackfriars Theatre opened by Burbage. Donne on Cadiz expedition.
- 1598 Donne appointed Secretary to Egerton.
- 1599 Earl of Essex, former favourite of Queen Elizabeth, arrested for failure to carry out her policies in Ireland. The Globe Theatre built on south bank of the Thames.
- 1601 Following an attempted uprising, Earl of Essex beheaded for treason. Donne secretly gets married to Anne More and is dismissed from Egerton's service. He becomes M.P.
- 1603 Elizabeth dies; succeeded by James I of England. Plague in London. Donne is 31.
- 1605 Gunpowder plot. Arrest and execution of Guy Fawkes.
- 1611 Authorised (or King James') Version of the Bible. Donne's First Anniversarie printed
- 1614 Globe theatre rebuilt after fire in previous year. Donne elected M. P. for Taunton
- 1615 Donne becomes Church of England priest. Receives D.D. from Cambridge University
- 1616 Lectures on the circulation of the blood by William Harvey in London.
- 1617 Anne Donne dies.
- 1618 Sir Walter Raleigh executed.
- 1620 Pilgrim Fathers to Massachusetts in the Mayflower
- 1621 Donne Dean of St.Paul's Cathedral, London.
- 1625 James I dies. Charles I becomes king. Charles marries Henrietta Maria of France.
- 1628 John Bunyan born. Laud appointed Bishop of London. Buckingham assassinated.

1629   Charles I suspends Parliament.
1631   March 31: Donne dies.
1642   Civil War begins between Royalists and Parliamentary forces (August).
1646   Charles surrenders to the Scots
1649   Charles I executed. Abolition of monarchy and
1657   Cromwell refuses to be crowned king
         Marvell becomes Latin Secretary to Government
1658   Cromwell, the Lord Protector, dies.
1660   Restoration: Charles II returns to England

Exam Advice

For the AQA A Level exam the student is not required to mention context. Instead students are urged to consider the speaker's sense of who s/he is and the way in which the speaker's sense of identity is projected through language. Responses should be focused and coherent and include suitable terminology. They must also analyse the ways in which meanings are shaped in the poems. Students are required to choose a relevant poem, but are not required to compare it to the given text.

For the Edexcel A Level exam the student is required to present a critical evaluative argument, with sustained textual examples, while at the same time evaluating the effects of literary features. Appropriate terminology is required along with a sophisticated level of expression. Furthermore, the student needs to demonstrate a sophisticated understanding of the writer's craft and his or her response must contain a critical evaluation of the ways meanings are shaped in texts. Reference to significant contextual factors should also be made along with links between texts and contexts. However, the ability to compare is not assessed in the Edexcel exam though the student may make some comment on the differences or similarities of the poems chosen while constructing a coherent essay. What is vital, however, is that the student avoids building a complex integrated comparison.

In the past students have been required either to explore the ways in which constancy is presented in *Woman's Constancy* and in one other poem, or to explore the ways in which Donne uses extremes in *Holy Sonnet V* ('I am a little world') and in one other poem. Both tasks also required the student to relate their discussion to relevant contextual factors. For the task on Woman's Constancy students could have selected The Relic as their second poem and explored constancy as a reflection of contemporary attitudes to male/female relationships. For the task on *Holy Sonnet V* ('I am a little world') an appropriate second poem would have been *Song* ('Go and catch a falling star').

Finally, the best way to revise for any poetry exam is to return to the poems and read them aloud. Make notes after each reading on the sound effects, its verbal music. Consider its rhyme, rhythm, melody; the use of enjambment, assonance, alliteration, onomatopoeia; the blending of repetition, the slow/fast movement; whether it is harsh, discordant, sibilance, sotto, allegro, rhapsodic, lyrical, elegiac, upbeat, melancholy, staccato, dirge-like; its tone, mood, atmosphere, voice.

Exam Questions

When considering a response to an essay question it is sometimes useful to consider the speaker's identity; the poetic voice (the way in which the speaker's sense of identity is projected through language choices so as to give the impression of a distinct persona with a personal history and a set of beliefs and values); and the speaker's point of view (through which a version of reality is presented).

Read *The Apparition* and *The Flea*. Compare and contrast how the narrators' feelings are presented in these poems.

Read *The Good-morrow* and *Woman's Constancy*. Compare and contrast the treatment of love in these poems.

Compare and contrast how Donne vividly conveys the feelings of a spurned suitor in two or more poems.

Compare and contrast how Donne presents women in two or more poems.

How does Donne compare his lovers' royalty or holiness with that of kings or saints in *The Anniversary* and one other poem of your choice?

Examine how Donne presents views about relationships between lovers in *The Sun Rising* and one other poem of your choice.

Explore how Donne expresses love in the *Air and Angels* and one other poem of your choice.

Model Essay

Examine how Donne presents views about separation in *A Valediction: Forbidding Mourning* and one other poem of your choice.

In *A Valediction* and *Elegy 12: His Picture*, Donne presents views about separation, acknowledging how a physical parting will not change the love they have for one another, in fact the separation will be beneficial in that suffering will refine it. Both speakers directly address their lovers as they leave, reassuring their lovers of the strength of their relationship and its transcendental nature, thus presenting their love as ideal. In *His Picture*, the speaker leaves a picture of himself to act as a reminder for his lover of who she fell in love with, therefore using a physical object in order to keep their love alive. However, in *A Valediction* the speaker suggests that through their spirituality and connected souls, they will continue to love each other despite distance.

In both poems Donne explores the idea of a microcosm, conveying their love as transcendental, meaning that though physically separated, they will always have each other and their love will survive. In *A Valediction*, Donne uses the central conceit of a compass, and depicts himself and his lover as 'stiff twin compasses' so that even when separated they 'lean, and hearken after' each other; though one 'doth roam', they will always be inseparable and firmly attached. This image also conveys the great age of exploration and discovery, while expressing a sense of indestructible and everlasting unity between the lovers, suggesting their love exists regardless of physical distance. Donne concludes the poem by telling his lover that she 'makes me end where I begun' rounding off the metaphor with the promise of returning. This image depicts a compass completing a full circle which suggests their love is all encompassing and completes them. The 'circle' created by the drawing of the compass creates an image of unity and represents the eternity of their love within a circle of time. Their love cannot be broken because of its spiritual strength and lack of purely sensual things. This Platonic view contrasts with the view that love is reliant upon the physical. This idea of an elevated love creates an air of exclusivity and places them on an almost celestial level. Donne presents separation as something beneath both relationships, as separation will only alter a base, physical love.

Therefore both poems believe that their parting will only make their attachment stronger, and that despite changes that may occur, their love will still thrive. In *A Valediction*, Donne also uses similes to create the idea that separation will only expand the area of their unified souls, describing that their separation will not be a problem but 'an expansion, Like gold to airy thinness beat', which references the idea of alchemy present in the sixth and seventh stanza. This image overall, depicts their separation and how they will become apart physically, however the 'gold' will cover more distance so that their love is all-encompassing, and therefore, their love spreads through the air, thus it is now part of their atmosphere.

Though the speaker briefly mentions the physical aspects they will miss: the 'eyes, lips and hands to miss' - the tricolon and sibilance giving the line a soothing tone - the speaker carries on to say that this does not matter as their love transcends the physical.

In *His Picture*, the speaker gives his lover a picture as a memento as he leaves for a long journey. As he departs, he tells her that 'thine in my heart, where my soul dwells, shall dwell'. In this hyperbolic image Donne references the metaphysical idea of the everlasting soul. By asserting this initially, Donne goes on to construct his argument. A loose form of a syllogism is often used by Donne in his poetry and is mostly employed to have a persuasive effect on his listener, usually a lover. The speaker claims that he and his lover are able to negate the impact of separation as their love for each other remains eternal in their souls. Their souls remain connected, thus any change to their physical situation is not a cause for concern. At its most powerful, this implies that death, the ultimate separation, will not affect them either.

To lend his assertions even more weight, the speaker references the rest of society and their ignorance concerning true love. Donne distances his own loves presented in both poems from what might be referred to as base loves rooted in physical attraction. In *A Valediction*, Donne sneers at other people's love and dubs it 'dull sublunary lover's love'. The use the premodifier 'sublunary' connotes Aristotelian physics and mocks this different type of love as he implies it is susceptible to the fickle influence of the moon, thus something with as powerful an impact as physical separation is not something this other form of love will be able to withstand. This, once again, links to Plato's theory of love and creates a distinction between higher and lower love and while the moon may be fickle in terms of changeability, it is still a powerful and worshipped celestial body, and by asserting his relationship above it, the speaker gives himself and his lover an almost divine status.

In *His Picture*, Donne mockingly gives voice to the rest of society which may try and discourage his lover from her continued loyalty while he is away. Donne labels them 'rival fools', meaning those that cannot understand love beyond physical attraction. The speaker also conveys their love as mature, in that 'the milk which in love's childish state / Did nurse it; who now is grown strong enough'. Here the lexical field of mature love emphasise that 'childish' love is weak, and relies on physical appearance. The temporal 'now' shows how the lover's relationship has gained its maturity, and therefore the speaker and his lover are able to rise above the physical aspect of their relationship in this separation. The speaker uses images of eternity when describing how his lover is in his 'heart, where my [his] soul dwells.' And that their love 'twill be more / When we [they] are shadows both'. Here Donne suggests that though the body will age and decay, their love will remain as their love is eternal.

The speaker in *His Picture* also describes how his physical appearance will change. Donne uses repetitive plosive sounds such as 'body' and 'bones broken' which creates a harsh sound which references the harsh journey the speaker is about to embark on. This also hyperbolically depicts the mental and physical injuries he will suffer as a result of this trip. Donne also uses metaphors such as 'care's rash sudden hoariness o'erspread' referencing how both his mental and physical health will be affected by his journey. The mental 'cares' or worries he'll experience are characterised as storms such as the compound modifier 'weather-worn', which will have a physical impact. The lexical contrasts and rhyming couplet 'farewell' and 'dwell', create a dichotomy that illustrates the speaker acknowledging a physical parting and the spiritual transcendence he shares with his lover.

Creative Tasks

Write a poem, in the style of Donne, which either celebrates his work or is a response from an addressee in one of his poems. Or write a short play script based on one of the poems. It could be a monologue or a dialogue between characters.

Glossary

Aubade: a morning love song (as opposed to a serenade, which is in the evening), or a song or poem about lovers separating at dawn. The aubade grew in popularity with the metaphysical poets. See *The Sun Rising*.

Conceit: an extended metaphor with a complex logic that governs a poetic passage or entire poem. By juxtaposing, usurping and manipulating images and ideas in surprising ways, a conceit invites the reader into a more sophisticated understanding of an object of comparison.

Elegy: in ancient Greece the elegy was a type of poem written in elegiacs, i.e., a poem written in couplets. The Greeks used this form for inscriptions on tombstones, but Ovid and Catullus, Latin poets of the Augustan age, adapted the elegy to a variety of subjects, one of which was love. In many seventeenth-century English elegies, there is a return to the funerary theme, but in his use of the elegy Donne as well as other contemporary poets popularized the Ovidian conception of love.

Donne's Elegies are metrically a loose imitation of the elegiac meter, as found in Ovid's elegies. Generally speaking, Donne writes rhyming iambic pentameter couplets, which vary from the smooth to the rhythmically rough. Almost everywhere, of course, he allows himself metrical latitude.

Metaphor: a substitution via an analogy; a comparison which denotes in order to establish a resemblance.

Metre: iambic pentameter is a commonly used type of metrical line in traditional English poetry and verse drama. The term describes the rhythm that the words establish in that line, which is measured in small groups of syllables called 'feet'. The word 'iambic' refers to the type of foot that is used, known as the iamb, which in English is an unstressed syllable followed by a stressed syllable. The word 'pentameter' indicates that a line has five of these 'feet'.

The da-DUM of a human heartbeat is the most common example of this rhythm. A standard line of iambic pentameter is five iambic feet in a row: da DUM da DUM da DUM da DUM da DUM

For example:
× / × / × / × / × /
To swell the gourd, and plump the hazel shells

× / × / × / × / × /
But, soft! What light through yonder window breaks?

    Although strictly speaking, iambic pentameter refers to five iambs in a row (as above), in practice, poets vary their iambic pentameter a great deal, while maintaining the iamb as the most common foot. However, there are some conventions to these variations. Iambic pentameter must always contain only five feet, and the second foot is almost always an iamb. The first foot, in contrast, often changes by the use of inversion, which reverses the order of the syllables in the foot. The following line from Shakespeare's *Richard III* begins with an inversion:

/ × × / × / × / × /
Now is the winter of our discontent

    Iambic tetrameter refers to a line consisting of four iambic feet. The word 'tetrameter' simply means that there are four feet in the line; iambic tetrameter is a line comprising four iambs.

× / × / × / × /
Come live with me and be my love - Christopher Marlowe, *The Passionate Shepherd to His Love*

Petrarchan: Donne was a leading destroyer of the Petrarchan convention in love poetry, which was the fashion of writing verses expressing adoration of a lady without any expectation that the love could, or even should, be returned. The fashion had been more or less invented by Petrarch, the great Italian sonneteer who wrote dozens of love poems to Laura, a young lady he had glimpsed in church and with whom he certainly had no expectation of a love affair.

Simile: a comparison using like or as.

Sonnet: a 14 line poem with a particular rhyme scheme. The form was popular in the 17th century. There are different types of sonnet, such as the Petrarchan. This form is divided into two distinct parts. The first 8 lines are called the octave (or octet) and present a 'problem, idea, or situation', the following six lines are called the sestet and present an answer or some sort of comment on the problem presented in the octave.

Sonnets also had a standard metre: iambic pentameter, which means alternating stress on the words, five stresses per line, yet Donne did not stick to the Petrarchan form. For a start, the rhyme scheme of a standard Petrarchan poem is 'abbaabba cdecde'. Donne's poems are often slightly different. For example, 'abcaabba dedeff'.

Donne also employed enjambment, the technique of running one line into another which adds to the emotional effect of a poem, in the octet.

Donne's sonnets are sometimes described as 'rough' for these reasons, but Donne had a clear purpose every time he 'broke the rules' of strict sonnet form - it adds to the emotional intensity of his argument and makes it stronger.

Trochaic tetrameter is a meter in poetry. It refers to a line of four trochaic feet. The word tetrameter simply means that the poem has four trochees. Unlike an iamb, a trochee is a long syllable, or stressed syllable, followed by a short, or unstressed, one.

Donne's Reputation

Critics by the end of the 17th century, such as John Dryden and Alexander Pope, were criticising Donne's poetry for the lack of regularity in its rhythm and its sexual content. Dryden first used the term 'metaphysical' to criticize Donne's 'excessive use of philosophy,' and Samuel Johnson used it to describe poets who wrote to 'show their learning.' Johnson also criticized Donne for what became known as the 'metaphysical conceit,' in which (says Johnson) 'the most heterogeneous ideas are joked by violence together.' As a result, by the 18th century, John Donne as a poet was forgotten. Although Romantics such as Samuel Coleridge and Charles Lamb began to rediscover the beauty in Donne's verse, it was not until the twentieth century that John Donne was resurrected as one of the greatest of English poets. This was in large part due to T. S. Eliot's essay *The Metaphysical Poets* (1921), which praised that which Dryden and Johnson condemned. Eliot argued that Donne's poetry possesses a capacity to synthesize emotional and intellectual experience so that the reader can 'feel...thought as immediately as the odour of a rose.' Throughout the middle of the 20th century, critics studied Donne to understand the tension, paradox, and ambiguity in his poetry; with some feminist critics arguing that his theme of mutuality in love even suggests a degree of equality.

Therefore, to briefly summarise, Donne was disliked throughout the 18th, admired in the 19th by a discerning minority, including Coleridge and Browning, and admired and elevated into a central and valued figure in the 20th. However, until recently Donne's reputation was underwritten by the facts that modern poets, such as Eliot, had seen him as useful and somehow contemporary. In contrast, this century had started with a genuine and widespread interest in his poetry and an interest in the Metaphysicals ability to wed widely separated ideas, and to make odd scraps of newly discovered knowledge serve immemorial themes.

Donne's Amatory Poems

Donne, while being one of the most highly regarded poets in English literature was also, at least as a young man, one of the most erotic. This clearly had something to do with him being a rake and a bawd before he became the dean of St. Paul's Cathedral. According to a contemporary source he was 'a great visitor of ladies' and 'a great writer of conceited verses.' He wrote poetry throughout his chequered, picaresque career and the range of the work that survives includes not only canonical love poems like *A Valediction: Forbidding Mourning* but erotica both intricate and raw. From *Elegy XVIII: Love's Progress* we get:

Her swelling lips; to which when we are come,
We anchor there, and think ourselves at home,
For they seem all: there sirens' songs, and there
Wise Delphic oracles do fill the ear;
There in a creek where chosen pearls do swell,
The remora, her cleaving tongue doth dwell.
These, and the glorious promontory, her chin
O'erpast; and the strait Hellespont between
The Sestos and Abydos of her breasts,
(Not of two lovers, but two loves the nests)
Succeeds a boundless sea, but that thine eye
Some island moles may scattered there descry;
And sailing towards her India, in that way
Shall at her fair Atlantic navel stay;
Though thence the current be thy pilot made,
Yet ere thou be where thou wouldst be embayed,
Thou shalt upon another forest set,
Where some do shipwreck, and no further get.
When thou art there, consider what this chase
Misspent by thy beginning at the face.

      He could also be highly suggestive, some might even say lewd. The following excerpt from *Elegy VIII: The*

Comparison gives, through similes, a vivid almost disturbing image:

Such cherishing heat her best loved part doth hold.
Thine's like the dread mouth of a fired gun,
Or like hot liquid metals newly run
Into clay moulds, or like to that Etna,
Where round about the grass is burnt away.

Donne's sexual interests were broad and in Sappho to Philaenis he explores the relationship between the Ancient Greek poet Sappho and her partner Phinaenis. Here he considers same-sex attraction:

Hand to strange hand, lip to lip none denies;
Why should they breast to breast, or thighs to thighs?
Likeness begets such strange self flattery,
That touching myself, all seems done to thee.
Myself I embrace, and my own hands I kiss,
And amorously thank myself for this.

Donne's career as a ladies' man ended after he met Anne More. He became a devoted husband, father of twelve (seven survived), and the author of mature love poems such as *The Sun Rising*, *The Canonization*, and *To His Mistress Going to Bed*, the latter lauded by David Malouf in his book *The Happy Life*: His celebration of his mistress's body is free, happy, entirely without shame or guilt, and expresses itself in language so active and sensual that it not only reproduces, as far as language can, his own energy and excitement, but attempts to transfer that energy, with its kinetic rhythms, to us as we read:

Licence my roving hands, and let them go
Behind, before, above, between, below.
Oh my America! my new-found-land.

The Mind of John Donne by Arthur Symons (1917)

Donne's mind was the mind of the dialectician (a philosopher who engages in the interaction of opposites), of the intellectual adventurer; he is a poet almost by accident, or at least for reasons with which art in the abstract has but little to do. He writes verse, first of all, because he has observed keenly, and because it pleases the pride of his intellect to satirise the pretensions of humanity. Then it is the flesh which speaks in his verse, the curiosity of woman, which he has explored in the same spirit of adventure; then passion, making a slave of him for love's sake, and turning at last to the slave's hatred; finally, religion, taken up with the same intellectual interest, the same subtle indifference, and, in its turn, passing also into passionate reality. A few poems are inspired in him by what he has seen in remote countries; some are marriage songs and funeral elegies, written for friendship or for money. But he speaks, in a letter, of 'descending to print anything in verse'; and it is certain that he was never completely absorbed by his own poetry, or at all careful to measure his achievements against those of others. He took his own poems very seriously, he worked upon them with the whole force of his intellect; but to himself, even before he became a divine, he was something more than a poet. Poetry was but one means of expressing the many-sided activity of his mind and temperament. Prose was another, preaching another; travel and contact with great events and persons scarcely less important to him, in the building up of himself.

And he was interested in everything. At one moment he is setting himself to study Oriental languages, a singularly difficult task in those days. Both in poetry and divinity he has more Spanish than English books in his library. Scientific and technical terms are constantly found in his verse, where we should least expect them, where indeed they are least welcome. He rebukes himself for his abandonment to 'the worst voluptuousness, which is an hydroptic, immoderate desire of human learning and languages.' At twenty-three he was a soldier against Spain under Raleigh, and went on the

'Islands Voyage'; later on, at different periods, he travelled over many parts of the Continent, with rich patrons or on diplomatic offices. Born a Catholic, he became a Protestant, deliberately enough; wrote books on controversial subjects, against his old party, before he had taken orders in the Church of England; besides a strange, morbid speculation on the innocence of suicide. He used his lawyer's training for dubious enough purposes, advising the Earl of Somerset in the dark business of his divorce and re-marriage. And, in a mournful pause in the midst of many harrowing concerns, he writes to a friend: 'When I must shipwreck, I would fain do it in a sea where mine own impotency might have some excuse; not in a sullen, weedy lake, where I could not have so much as exercise for my swimming. Therefore I would fain do something, but that I cannot tell what is no wonder.' 'Though I be in such a planetary and erratic fortune that I can do nothing constantly,' he confesses later in the same letter.

No doubt some of this feverish activity, this uncertainty of aim, was a matter of actual physical health. It is uncertain at what time the wasting disease, of which he died, first settled upon him; but he seems to have been always somewhat sickly of body, and with just that at times depressing, at times exciting, malady which tells most upon the whole organisation. That preoccupation with death, which in early life led him to write his *Biathanatos*, with its elaborate apology for suicide, and at the end of his life to prepare so spectacularly for the act of dying, was but one symptom of a morbid state of body and brain and nerves, to which so many of his poems and so many of his letters bear witness. 'Sometimes,' he writes, in a characteristic letter, 'when I find myself transported with jollity and love of company, I hang lead to my heels, and reduce to my thoughts my fortunes, my years, the duties of a man, of a friend, of a husband, of a father, and all the incumbencies of a family; when sadness dejects me, either I countermine it with another sadness, or I kindle squibs about me again, and fly into sportfulness and company.'

At the age of thirty-five he writes from his bed describing every detail of what he frantically calls 'a sickness which I cannot name or describe,' and ends his letter: 'I profess to you truly, that my loathness to give over now, seems to myself an ill sign that I shall write no more.' It was at this time that he wrote the *Biathanatos*, with its explicit declaration in the preface: 'Whensoever any affliction assails me, methinks I have the keys of my prison in mine own hand, and no remedy presents itself so soon to my heart as mine own sword.' Fifteen years later, when one of his most serious illnesses was upon him, and his life in real danger, he notes down all his symptoms as he lies awake night after night, with an extraordinary and, in itself, morbid acuteness. 'I observe the physician with the same diligence as he the disease; I see he fears, and I fear with him; I overtake him, I over-run him in his fear, because he makes his pace slow; I fear the more because he disguises his fear, and I see it with the more sharpness because he would not have me see it.'

As he lies in bed, he realises 'I am mine own ghost, and rather affright my beholders than instruct them. They conceive the worst of me now, and yet fear worse; they give me for dead now, and yet wonder how I do when they wake at midnight, and ask how I do to-morrow. Miserable and inhuman posture, where I must practise my lying in the grave by lying still.' This preying upon itself of the brain is but one significant indication of a temperament, neurotic enough indeed, but in which the neurosis is still that of the curious observer, the intellectual casuist, rather than of the artist. A wonderful piece of self-analysis, worthy of St. Augustine, which occurs in one of his funeral sermons, gives poignant expression to what must doubtless have been a common condition of so sensitive a brain. 'I throw myself down in my chamber, and I call in and invite God and His angels together; and when they are there, I neglect God and his angels for the noise of a fly, for the rattling of a coach, for the whining of a door; I talk on in the same posture of prayer, eyes lifted up, knees bowed down, as though I prayed to God; and if God should ask me when I last thought of God in that prayer, I cannot tell. Sometimes I find that I forgot what I was about; But when I began to forget it, I cannot tell. A memory of yesterday's pleasures, a fear of to-morrow's dangers, a straw under my knee, a noise in mine ear, a chimera in my brain, troubles me in my prayer.' It is this brain, turned inward upon itself, and darting out on every side in purely random excursions, that was responsible, I cannot doubt, for all the contradictions of a career in which the inner logic is not at first apparent.

Donne's Career by Arthur Symons (1917)

Donne's career divides itself sharply into three parts: his youth, when we see him as a soldier, a traveller, a lover, a poet, unrestrained in all the passionate adventures of youth; then a middle period, in which he is a lawyer and a theologian, seeking knowledge and worldly advancement, without any too restraining scruple as to the means which come to his hand; and then a last stage of saintly living and dying. He was indeed all of these, and his individuality grew from one stage to another, the subtle intelligence being always there, working vividly. 'I would fain do something, but that I cannot tell what is no wonder.' Everything in Donne seems to explain itself in that fundamental uncertainty of aim, and his uncertainty of aim partly by a morbid physical condition. He searches, nothing satisfies him, tries everything, in vain; finding satisfaction at last in the Church, as in a haven of rest. Always it is the curious, insatiable brain searching. And he is always wretchedly aware that he 'can do nothing constantly.'

His three periods, then, are three stages in the search after a way to walk in, something worthy of himself to do. Thus, of his one printed collection of verse he writes: 'Of my *Anniversaries*, the fault which I acknowledge in myself is to have descended to print anything in verse, which, though it have excuse, even in our times, by example of men, which one would think should as little have done it as I, yet I confess I wonder how I declined to it, and do not pardon myself.' Of his legal studies he writes in the same letter: 'For my purpose of proceeding in the profession of the law, so far as to a title, you may be pleased to correct that imagination where you find it. I ever thought the study of it my best entertainment and pastime, but I have no ambition nor design upon the style.' Until he accepts religion, with all its limitations and encouragements, he has not even sure landmarks on his way.

From that time to the end of his life he had found what he had all the while been seeking: rest for the restlessness of his mind, in a meditation upon the divine nature; occupation, in being 'ambassador of God,' through the pulpit; himself, as it seemed to him, at his fullest and noblest. It was himself, really, that he had been seeking all the time, conscious at least of that in all the deviations of the way; himself, the ultimate of his curiosities.

And yet, what remains to us out of this life of many purposes, which had found an end satisfying to itself in the Deanery of St. Paul's, is simply a bundle of manuscript verses, which the writer could bring himself neither to print nor to destroy. His first satire speaks contemptuously of 'giddy fantastic poets,' and, when he allowed himself to write poetry, he was resolved to do something different from what anybody had ever done before, not so much from the artist's instinctive desire of originality, as from a kind of haughty, yet really bourgeois, desire to be indebted to nobody. 'He began,' said one critic 'as if poetry had never been written before.'

Donne's Poetry and Prose by Robert Lynd (1921)

One cannot, unfortunately, write the history of the progress of Donne's genius save by inference and guessing. His poems were not, with some unimportant exceptions, published in his lifetime. He did not arrange them in chronological or in any sort of order. His poem on the flea that has bitten both him and his inamorata comes after the triumphant *Anniversary* and but a page or two before the *Nocturnal upon St. Lucy's Day*. Hence there is no means of telling how far we are indebted to the Platonism of one woman, how much to his marriage with another, for the enrichment of his genius. Such a poem as *The Canonization* can be interpreted either in a Platonic sense or as a poem written to Anne More, who was to bring him both imprisonment and the liberty of love. It is, in either case, written in defence of his love against some who censured him for it: 'For God's sake, hold your tongue, and let me love.' In the last two verses of the poem Donne proclaims that his love cannot be measured by the standards of the vulgar:

We can die by it, if not live by love,
And if unfit for tombs and hearse
Our legend be, it will be fit for verse;
And if no piece of chronicle we prove,
We'll build in sonnets pretty rooms;
As well a well-wrought urn becomes
The greatest ashes, as half-acre tombs,
And by these hymns, all shall approve
Us canonized for Love.

And thus invoke us: 'You, whom reverend love
Made one another's hermitage;
You, to whom love was peace, that now is rage;
Who did the whole world's soul contract, and drove
Into the glasses of your eyes
(So made such mirrors, and such spies,
That they did all to you epitomize)
Countries, towns, courts: beg from above
A pattern of your love!'

According to Walton, it was to his wife that Donne addressed the beautiful verses beginning: 'Sweetest love, I do not go / For weariness of thee'; as well as the series of Valedictions. Of many of the other love-poems, however, we can measure the intensity but not guess the occasion. All that we can say with confidence when we have read them is that, after we have followed one tributary on another leading down to the ultimate Thames of his genius, we know that his progress as a lover was a progress from infidelity to fidelity, from wandering amorousness to deep and enduring passion. The image that is finally stamped on his greatest work is not that of a roving adulterer, but of a monotheist of love. It is true that there is enough Don-Juanism in the poems to have led at least one critic to think of Donne's verse rather as a confession of his sins than as a golden book of love.

Yet to the modern reader there is as much divinity in the best of the love-poems as in the best of the religious ones. Donne's last word as a secular poet may well be regarded as having been uttered in that great poem in celebration of lasting love, *The Anniversary*, which closes with so majestic a sweep:

Here upon earth we are kings, and none but we
Can be such kings, nor of such subjects be.
Who is so safe as we, where none can do
Treason to us, except one of us two?
True and false fears let us refrain;
Let us love nobly, and live, and add again
Years and years unto years, till we attain
To write three-score: this is the second of our reign.

Donne's conversion as a lover was obviously as complete and revolutionary as his conversion in religion. It is said, indeed, to have led to his conversion to passionate religion. When his marriage with Sir George More's sixteen-year-old daughter brought him at first only imprisonment and poverty, he summed up the sorrows of the situation in the famous line - a line which has some additional interest as suggesting the correct pronunciation of his name:

John Donne; Anne Donne; Undone.

His married life, however, in spite of a succession of miseries due to ill-health, debt and thwarted ambition, seems to have been happy beyond prophecy; and when at the end of sixteen years his wife died in childbed, after having borne him twelve children, a religious crisis resulted that turned his conventional churchmanship into sanctity. His original change from Catholicism to Protestantism has been already mentioned. Most are agreed, however, that this was a conversion in a formal rather than in a spiritual sense. Even when he took Holy Orders in 1615, at the age of forty-two, he appears to have done so less in answer to any impulse to a religious life from within but because all hope of advancement through his legal attainments had been brought to an end. And after his admission into the Church he reveals himself as ungenerously morose when the Countess of Bedford, in trouble about her own extravagances, can afford him no more than £30 to pay his debts. The truth is, to be forty and a failure is an affliction that might sour even a healthy nature. The effect on a man of Donne's ambitious and melancholy temperament, together with the memory of his dissipated health and his dissipated fortune, and the spectacle of a long family in constant process of increase, must have been disastrous. To such a man poverty and neglected merit are a prison. Shakespeare and Shelley had in them some volatile element that could, one feels, have escaped through the bars and sung above the ground.

In his poems and letters Donne is haunted especially by three images: the hospital, the prison, and the grave. Disease, I think, preyed on his mind even more terrifyingly than warped ambition. 'Put all the miseries that man is subject to together,' he exclaims in one of the passage from the Sermons, 'sickness is more than all... In poverty I lack but other things; in banishment I lack but other men; but in sickness I lack myself.' Walton declares that it was from consumption that Donne suffered; but he had probably the seeds of many diseases. In some of his letters he dwells miserably on the symptoms of his illnesses. At one time, his sickness 'hath so much of a cramp that it wrests the sinews, so much of tetane that it withdraws and pulls the mouth, and so much of the gout... that it is not like to be cured... I shall,' he adds, 'be in this world, like a porter in a great house, but seldomest abroad; I shall have many things to make me weary, and yet not get leave to be gone.' Even after his conversion he felt drawn to a morbid insistence on the details of his ill-health. Those amazing records which he wrote while lying ill in bed in October, 1623, give us a realistic study of a sick-bed and its circumstances, the gloom of which is hardly even lightened by his odd account of the disappearance of his sense of taste: 'My taste is not gone away, but gone up to sit at David's table; my stomach is not gone, but gone upwards toward the Supper of the Lamb.' 'I am mine own ghost,' he cries, 'and rather affright my beholders than interest them... Miserable and inhuman fortune, when I must practise my lying in the grave by lying still.'

It does not surprise one to learn that a man thus assailed by wretchedness and given to looking in the mirror of his own bodily corruptions was often tempted, by 'a sickly inclination,' to commit suicide, and that he even wrote, though he did not dare to publish, an apology for suicide on religious grounds, his famous and little-read *Biathanatos*. The family crest of the Donnes was a sheaf of snakes, and these symbolize well enough the brood of temptations that twisted about in this unfortunate Christian's bosom. Donne, in the days of his salvation, abandoned the family crest for a new one: Christ crucified on an anchor. But he might well have left the snakes writhing about the anchor. He remained a tempted man to the end.

One wishes that the Sermons threw more light on his later personal life than they do. But perhaps that is too much to expect of sermons. There is no form of literature less personal except a leading article. The preacher usually regards himself as a mouthpiece rather than a man giving expression to himself. In the circumstances what surprises us is that the Sermons reveal, not so little, but so much of Donne. Indeed, they make us feel far more intimate with Donne than do his private letters, many of which are little more than exercises in composition. As a preacher, no less than as a poet, he is inflamed by the creative heat. He shows the same vehemence of fancy in the presence of the divine and infernal universe - a vehemence that prevents even his most far-sought extravagances from disgusting us as do the lukewarm follies of the Euphuists. Undoubtedly the modern reader smiles when Donne, explaining that man can be an enemy of God as the mouse can be an enemy to the elephant, goes on to speak of 'God who is not only a multiplied elephant, millions of elephants multiplied into one, but a multiplied world, a multiplied all, all that can be conceived by us, infinite many times over; nay (if we may dare to say so) a multiplied God, a God that hath the millions of the heathens' gods in Himself alone.' But at the same time one finds oneself taking a serious pleasure in the huge sorites of quips and fancies in which he loves to present the divine argument. Nine out of ten readers of the Sermons, I imagine, will be first attracted to them through love of the poems. They need not be surprised if they do not immediately enjoy them. The dust of the pulpit lies on them thickly enough. As one goes on reading them, however, one becomes suddenly aware of their florid and exiled beauty. One sees beyond their local theology to the passion of a great suffering artist. Here are sentences that express the Paradise, the Purgatory, and the Hell of John Donne's soul. A noble imagination is at work, a grave-digging imagination, but also an imagination that is at home among the stars. Listen to this, for example, from a sermon preached in St. Paul's in January, 1626:

Let me wither and wear out mine age in a discomfortable, in an unwholesome, in a penurious prison, and so pay my debts with my bones, and recompense the wastefulness of my youth with the beggary of mine age; let me wither in a spittle under sharp, and foul, and infamous diseases, and so recompense the wantonness of my youth with that loathsomeness in mine age; yet, if God withdraw not his spiritual blessings, his grace, his patience, if I can call my suffering his doing, my passion his action, all this that is temporal, is but a caterpillar got into one corner of my garden, but a mildew fallen upon one acre of my corn: the body of all, the substance of all is safe, so long as the soul is safe.

The self-contempt with which his imagination loved to intoxicate itself finds more lavish expression in a passage in a sermon delivered on Easter Sunday two years later:

When I consider what I was in my parents' loins (a substance unworthy of a word, unworthy of a thought), when I consider what I am now (a volume of diseases bound up together; a dry cinder, if I look for natural, for radical moisture; and yet a sponge, a bottle of overflowing Rheums, if I consider accidental; an aged child, a grey-headed infant, and but the ghost of mine own youth), when I consider what I shall be at last, by the hand of death, in my grave (first, but putrefaction, and, not so much as putrefaction; I shall not be able to send forth so much as ill air, not any air at all, but shall be all insipid, tasteless, savourless, dust; for a while, all worms, and after a while, not so much as worms, sordid, senseless, nameless dust), when I consider the past, and present, and future state of this body, in this world, I am able to conceive, able to express the worst that can befall it in nature, and the worst that can be inflicted on it by man, or fortune. But the least degree of glory that God hath prepared for that body in heaven, I am not able to express, not able to conceive.

Excerpts of great prose seldom give us that rounded and final beauty which we expect in a work of art; and the reader of Donne's Sermons in their latest form will be wise if he comes to them expecting to find beauty piecemeal and tarnished though in profusion. Even as it is, there is no other Elizabethan man of letters whose personality is an island with a crooked shore, inviting us into a thousand bays and creeks and river-mouths, to the same degree as the personality that expressed itself in the poems, sermons, and life of John Donne. It is a mysterious and at times repellent island. It lies only intermittently in the sun. A fog hangs around its coast, and at the base of its most radiant mountain-tops there is, as a rule, a miasma-infested swamp. There are jewels to be found scattered among its rocks and over its surface, and by miners in the dark. It is richer, indeed, in jewels and precious metals and curious ornaments than in flowers. The shepherd on the hillside seldom tells his tale uninterrupted. Strange rites in honour of ancient infernal deities that delight in death are practised in hidden places, and the echo of these reaches him on the sighs of the wind and makes him shudder even as he looks at his beloved. It is an island with a cemetery smell. The chief figure who haunts it is a living man in a winding-sheet.

It is, no doubt, Walton's story of the last days of Donne's life that makes us, as we read even the sermons and the love-poems, so aware of this ghostly apparition. Donne, it will be remembered, almost on the eve of his death, dressed himself in a winding-sheet, 'tied with knots at his head and feet,' and stood on a wooden urn with his eyes shut, and 'with so much of the sheet turned aside as might show his lean, pale, and death-like face,' while a painter made a sketch of him for his funeral monument. He then had the picture placed at his bedside, to which he summoned his friends and servants in order to bid them farewell. As he lay awaiting death, he said characteristically, 'I were miserable if I might not die,' and then repeatedly, in a faint voice, 'Thy Kingdom come, Thy will be done.'

At the very end he lost his speech, and 'as his soul ascended and his last breath departed from him he closed his eyes, and then disposed his hands and body into such a posture as required not the least alteration by those that came to shroud him.'

It was a strange chance that preserved his spectral monument almost uninjured when St. Paul's was burned down in the Great Fire, and no other monument in the cathedral escaped. Among all his fantasies none remains in the imagination more despotically than this last fanciful game of dying. Donne, however, remained in all respects a fantastic to the last, as we may see in that hymn which he wrote eight days before the end, tricked out with queer geography, and so anciently egoistic amid its worship, as in the verse:

Whilst my physicians by their love are grown
Cosmographers, and I their map, who lie

Flat on this bed, that by them may be shown
That this is my south-west discovery,
Per fretum febris, by these straits to die.

Donne was the poet-geographer of himself, his mistresses, and his God. Other poets of his time dived deeper and soared to greater altitudes, but none travelled so far, so curiously, and in such out-of-the-way places, now hurrying like a nervous fugitive, and now in the exultation of the first man in a new found land.

Biographies on Donne

Biography as a fine art can go no further, according to Arthur Symons (writing in the early twentieth century), than Walton's *Life and Death of Dr Donne*. From the 'good and virtuous parents' of the first line to the 'small quantity of Christian dust' of the last, every word is the touch of a cunning brush painting a picture. 'The picture lives, and with so vivid and gracious a life that it imposes itself upon us as the portrait of a real man, faithfully copied from the man as he lived. But that is precisely the art of the painter. Walton's picture is so beautiful because everything in it is sacrificed to beauty; because it is a convention, a picture in which life is treated almost as theme for music.'

For a life of Donne, which makes no pretence to harmonise a sometimes discordant existence, Symons also recommends Gosse's *Life and Letters of John Donne, Dean of St. Paul's*. According to Symons: 'it begins with the eager, attractive, somewhat homely youth of eighteen, grasping the hilt of his sword so tightly that his knuckles start out from the thin covering of flesh before passing into the mature Donne, the lean, humorous, large-browed, courtly thinker, with his large intent eyes, a cloak folded elegantly about his uncovered throat, or the ruff tightening about his carefully trimmed beard; and ending with the ghastly emblem set as a frontispiece to Death's Duel the dying man wrapped already in his shroud, which gathers into folds above his head, as if tied together like the mouth of a sack, while the sunken cheeks and hollow closed eyelids are mocked by the shapely moustache, brushed upwards from the lips.'

A more recent biography is John Stubbs' *Donne, The Reformed Soul*. This is a scholarly work and gives the reader a clear picture of the poet's life and the period in which he lived. However, the reader must always return to the poems if s/he is to make sense of Donne and reading poems is usually, as Professor Burrow once remarked, a process of losing and finding one's balance, and then wondering if one has really grasped the thing after all. And remember, John Donne's poems in particular are extremely unstable and often argue implausible cases.

Bibliography

Erotic Poetry A Cambridge Companion to John Donne. Gibboury, Achsah. Cambridge: Cambridge University Press, 2006.

Gender Matters: The Women in Donne's Poems Bell, Ilona *The Cambridge Companion to John Donne.* Ed. Achsah Gibbourey. Cambridge: Cambridge University Press, 2006.

John Donne, Devotions upon Emergent Occasions Ed. Anthony Raspa. Montreal: McGill-Queen's University Press, 1975.

John Donne's Poetry. Arthur L. Clements, Ed. New York: W.W. Norton & Co., 1992.

Letters to Severall Persons of Honour (1651) A Collection of Letters, Made by Sr Tobie Mathews, Kt. (1660).

The Complete Poetry and Selected Prose of John Donne Ed. Charles M. Coffin New York: The Modern Library, 1952.

Olympia Harbour Publications Inc

Other Titles in the Critical Study Guide Series include:

A Critical Study Guide for the AQA English Language and Literature Paris Anthology
M Parks, 2017

Othello in Context – A Critical Study Guide for A Level English
M Parks, 2020

Dracula – A Critical Study Guide
L Steinmetz, 2016

Beowulf – Abridged for Schools and Colleges
T Chatterton, 2015

Frankenstein – A Critical Study Guide
J McLaine, 2015

Thomas Hardy's Poetry – A Critical Study Guide
J McLaine, 2015

Northanger Abbey – A Critical Study Guide
J McLaine, 2013

Tennyson's Poetry – A Critical Study Guide
T Halliwell-Grove, 2012

Olympia Harbour Publications Inc.
Marlinspike Building, Marlinspike Place, Greenwich, Conn.